Production Credits

Production Manager   **Simon Sturgess**
Deputy Stage Manager   **Natasha Gooden**
Assistant Stage Manager   **Kerry Sullivan**
Costume Supervisor   **Chrissy Madison**

Theatre Royal Stratford East – Special Thanks

Smeg Retro – 0844 557 9907
ARCAM
Stratford Library
John & Maria Sullivan
Marie Costa
La Cafetiere
Morphy Richards
NMG product placement
The Royal Academy of Music
Hackney Empire
Prontaprint, Stratford
The Marlborough Arms
RADA
Taylors of Harrogate
Sarah Appiah
Geeta Singh
Cast photos by Ila Desai

Thanks to Shazeaa Ingar for providing two pieces of original artwork.
Shazeaa is an Islamic calligraphy artist based both in the UK and
UAE. Her work is characterised by contemporary Arabic calligraphy
against a backdrop of vibrant, intense colours and textures inspired by
meaningful Qur'anic verses. shazeaaingar@hotmail.com

Interview with writer and actor Cosh Omar and director Kerry Michael

What is the play about?

CO: The play is about a young man who's desperately trying to cultivate himself out of his past and out of the surroundings he grew up in. But it's very hard to do because people keep catching up with him; his life keeps catching up with him, his family and the silly things he does.

KM: It's about identity and about how when two entities get together there's a fear of losing one's identity through compromise and how through compromise we lose our voice however in truth I believe we adapt and that's how we move on. We keep evolving, the way we look, the way we sound, the way we represent ourselves, the way we communicate. It's also about when and if Turkey joins the European Union and The West fearing a Muslim country being in its midst.

Sounds like you've touched on some very serious issues. How did you go about making the story funny?

CO: Well to me it was obviously going to be a comedy. I wanted to show the history of how Muslims have influenced Europe. But they didn't do that alone, within the Islamic world Jews played a big part. I wanted to use a voice that was different from the indigenous one and show a lot of the humour we inherited came from the Jewish community – from Yiddish theatres of Eastern Europe. To me it was obvious to use that voice in a comedy. I wrote it in that way to show the mutual history that Jews and Muslims share.

KM: I think also it's about a stewing tank where you just gather up all these characters in one space at one time and lock the door on them and the potential grows and grows until you get an outrageous situation.

Your first play, **The Battle of Green Lanes,** *caused quite a stir. Did you find there was much pressure on you to come back with a second offering?*

CO: Not really, because even with the success and buzz about *The Battle of Green Lanes* it was important for me to look at it and think – what is that buzz really all about? I'm really proud of it and that's great but when I've got something to say I say it. I did it then and it went well, then when I had something to say again I wrote another play.

What is it like to be performing in your own play?

CO: It's amazing, because it's one thing to create a world and then another to step into that world. Also because for me on a personal level, as an actor I'll only get cast as a terrorist, a Turkish mechanic or a kebab shop owner. For

THEATRE ROYAL
— STRATFORD EAST —

The Great Extension

By Cosh Omar

First performed at Theatre Royal Stratford East
on Friday 16th October 2009

Theatre Royal Stratford East
Gerry Raffles Square
Stratford
London
E15 1BN

www.stratfordeast.com

The Great Extension

By Cosh Omar

Cast
(in alphabetical order)

Mr Hassan	**Dimitri Andreas**
Abdul Aziz Khan	**Faraz Ayub**
Mrs Hassan	**Carol Been**
Policeman	**Ben Bennett**
Mr Brown	**Jack Chissick**
Newsreader	**Rebecca Deren**
Hamid Khan	**Amerjit Deu**
Handsome Turkish Man	**Akin Gazi**
Sanjay	**Raj Ghatak**
David	**Jacob Krichefski**
Hassan	**Cosh Omar**
Aisha Khan	**Sharona Sassoon**
Jamillia Khan	**Ruby Visaria**

Creative Team

Writer	**Cosh Omar**
Director	**Kerry Michael**
Set & Costumes Designer	**Yannis Thavoris**
Lighting Designer	**Prema Mehta**
Sound Designer	**Theo Holloway, Orbital Sound**
Assistant Director	**Matthew Blacklock**

me it's fantastic to create a world that I know there's truth to and to perform a part that I don't get to play normally. It's a very privileged position.

Can you tell us more about the vision TRSE has and how this play fulfils it?

KM: British Theatre is full of prejudice with so many invisible barriers – there is a really distrustful Old Boy network, so we do work for people who want an alternative to all of that. There's no point in doing the same thing as everyone else. I like to think that we'll do the plays that other people don't want to do. We want to find work which is really special, but no-one has worked that out yet.

What does the future hold for both of you?

KM: I'm really pleased to be doing his second play, but I think it will form part of a trilogy. So I'm looking forward to that.

CO: Sounds like I'll be writing another play! I'm very excited about producing another piece at Theatre Royal again.

What will your next play be about?

CO: I've no idea yet... I'd like to write more for a female voice, a female protagonist. But it's one that I've not worked out yet. It's not about what I want – it's seeing what goes on between now and then, how I process that and then I'll know how to convey it. As an actor and as a writer I'm loath to predict – I'd rather go with the flow. Sometimes it's colourful and sometimes it's dark.

Cast in Alphabetical Order

Dimitri Andreas **Mr Hassan**

Dimitri's first foray into acting was in 1956 at the age of 13 when he was talent spotted in Soho and appeared as Nico in *Ill Met by Moonlight* with Dirk Bogarde, a Powell and Pressburger Film. Dimitri was a founding member of the Theatro Technic which had a close association with Joan Littlewood's Theatre Workshop at the Theatre Royal Stratford East. He then went on to Webber Douglas School of Drama from 1959 to 1961 and has continued in film, theatre and television. His most memorable theatre work was at the Royal Court in Arnold Wesker's *The Kitchen* and the West End stage production *Talking to You* by William Saroyan. Most recent film and television productions include *Layer Cake*, *Faith* and *Prince of Persia*.

Faraz Ayub **Abdul Aziz Khan**

Born and Raised in the Midlands, Faraz Ayub got his first taste for acting while performing at local workshops run by Carlton Television. After appearing in several international award winning short films, Faraz decided to make the move to London where he began his training at the Zoë Nathenson School of Acting. The past year has been particularly good to Faraz with a starring role in a film directed by Kole Onlie Ere, and a guest role in the new series of the BBC's *Spooks*. *The Great Extension* is Faraz's first major appearance in a London theatre.

Carol Been **Mrs Hassan**

Carol trained at Guildhall School of Music and Drama. Theatre includes: *'Tis Pity She's A Whore* at the Royal National Theatre and various productions at Harrogate Theatre, Riverside Coleraine, Old Red Lion, The Gate Theatre, The Drill Hall Theatre, Battersea Arts Centre, Bloomsbury Theatre and Edinburgh Fringe Festival. Television and Film includes: *The Brief*, *Closing Ranks*, *Footballers' Wives*, *Kissing Buba*, *The Undertakers*, *Crime Limited*. Carol is also a fully qualified exercise instructor.

Ben Bennett **Policeman**

Ben Bennett was last seen on the Stratford East stage in Paulette Randall's 'Urban Afro Saxons' in 2003. A graduate of The Bristol Old Vic Theatre School he has also played in many other successful productions around the country: Mustapha Matura's *Three Sisters* (Birmingham Rep and National Tour); *At The Gates of Gaza* by Juliet Gilkes Romero (National Tour) and the 20th anniversary revival of *Playboy of the West Indies* at the Tricycle Theatre. Ben also teaches drama and is studying theatre direction.

Jack Chissick **Mr Brown**

This year's Theatre: The British Premiere of *Beau Jeste* (Hackney Empire), the World Premiere of Caryl Churchill's *Seven Jewish Children* (Royal Court Theatre), *Soho Streets* (Soho Theatre). Snout in *Fairy Queen* (Glyndebourne opera) and later this year and next to be seen in New York and Paris. Jack's previous Theatre Royal credits include: *Better Times* and *Fatty*.
Television includes: *Casualty 1907* (BBC), *Holby City* (BBC), *Silent Witness* (BBC), *The Bill* (Talkback Thames), *Coronation Street* (Granada), *The Worst Week of My Life* (Tiger Aspect), *Fruitcake of the Living Dead* (BBC), *Canterbury Tales: The Pardoner's Tale* (BBC), *Foyle's War II* (Greenlit Productions), *Grass* (BBC), *Heartbeat* (Yorkshire Television), *Peter Ackroyd's London* (BBC), *'Orrible* (BBC), *Midsomer Murders* (Bentley Productions).
Film includes: *Somerstown*, *Escape from Sobibor*, *Spoils*, *Entrapment*, *Van Gogh's Ear*, *Future Shock*, *A Kind of Hush*, *Emma*, *Restoration*.

Amerjit Deu **Hamid Khan**

Amerjit trained at Webber Douglas Academy of Dramatic Art. Credits include *Seven Other Children* (New End Theatre), *Heer Ranjha* (Tramway Theatre Glasgow), *Frost Nixon* (Donmar Warehouse and Gielgud Theatre), *Zameen* (Kali Theatre), *Twelfth Night* (British Council), *Only When I Laugh* (Derek Nimmo tour of the world), *Fourteen Emotions* (Drill Hall), *Dr Faustus* (Nuffield Theatre Southampton), *Clerical Outfitters* (Dukes Playhouse Lancaster).

Television includes: *Harley Street*, *Doctors*, *Casualty*, *The Swap*, *Silent Witness*, *Waking the Dead*, *Holby City*, *Murder City*, *Udam Singh*, *Eldorado*, *EastEnders*. He will soon be seen in *Identity*, *Cast Offs* (CH4) and *Londoners*.

Film includes: *Bend it like Beckham*, *Lasko*, *Bollywood Queen*, *The Biographer*, *Mad Cows*, *Food of Love*, *Guru in Seven*, *Deceivers*.

Radio includes: *Torchwood*, *The Razor's Edge*, *Number 10* and *Silver Street*.

Akin Gazi **Handsome Turkish Man**

Akin Gazi studied at Queen Mary & Westfield College, University of London, gaining a BA in English & Drama. After qualifying he was repeatedly told that pursuing an acting career was madness and ill advised. Ignoring that he wrote and performed the one man show *I'm Not Racist But* at the Space Theatre and *The Master Plan*, a play for children about aliens that travel to Earth to find Jennifer Lopez. He played *Ziah* in feature film *The Convert* and has had guest roles in various TV programmes including the ABC mini-series *The Path to 9/11*, ITV's *The Bill* and the BBC's *Dead Ringers* & *Doctor Who*. He also performed for the Para-site theatre company in the site-specific piece *The White Room*, playing the chronic insomniac and delusional *A*.

Raj Ghatak **Sanjay**

Raj trained at the Central School of Speech and Drama and Queen Mary University.

Theatre includes: *The Spiral* (The Royal Court Theatre), *Simply Cinderella* (The Curve), *Free Outgoing* (The Royal Court Theatre), *Tales From Firozsha Baag* (National Theatre Studio), *High Heel Parrotfish* (Theatre Royal Stratford East), *Bombay Dreams* (Apollo Victoria, West End), *Hijra* (Bush/West Yorkshire Playhouse), *Side Story* (Prince of Wales Theatre, West End), *East is East* (Oldham Coliseum), *Don't Look at my Sister Innit!* (Bloomsbury Theatre/Watermans), *Nagwanti* (Tara Arts).

Television includes: Grayson in Charlie Brooker's *Dead Set* (E4 and C4. BAFTA winner and BAFTA nominated for Best Drama Serial), *Doctors (BBC)*, *Sinchronicity* (BBC), *All About Me* (Celador), *Hard Cash* (BBC), *Out of Sight* (Carlton).

Film includes: *Karma Magnet, Dangerous Parking, Starter for 10, The Lives of the Saints, Birthday Girl, Sari and Trainers*.
Awards: Nominated for Best Actor (2004) and Best Supporting Performance in a Musical for *Bombay Dreams*.

Jacob Krichefski **David**

Jacob trained at Webber Douglas.
Television includes: *A Touch of Frost* (Yorkshire), *Silent Witness* (BBC Television), *The Bill* (ITV), *Sex Traffic* (CH4), *Casualty* (BBC), *Family Affairs* (CH5), *Maisie Raine* (BBC), *Iechyd Da* (S4C), *Preston Front* (BBC).
Theatre includes: *The Seagull* (The Factory), *The Tempest* (York Theatre Royal / Sprite), *The Hamlet Project* (The Factory), *Lucifer Saved* (Finborough Theatre), *2000yrs* (National theatre), *Market Boy* (National Theatre).
Radio includes: *The Kiss - The Advertiser* (BBC Radio 4).

Cosh Omar **Hassan**

Cosh trained at ALRA. Theatre includes: *Baghdad Wedding* (Soho Theatre), *The Battle Of Green Lanes* (Theatre Royal Stratford East), *Macbeth* (Arcola Theatre), *'100'* (Arcola Theatre), *A Midsummer Night's Dream* (Arcola Theatre), *Murder* (Gate Theatre), *Rosencrantz & Guildenstern are Dead* (Arcola Theatre), *Shrewd* (Arcola Theatre).
Screen work includes: *The Bill* (Thames Television), *Bleak House* (BBC Television), *EastEnders* (BBC Television), *Murder Prevention* (World Productions, Channel 5), *Spooks 3* (Kudos Productions/BBC), *Ultimate Force II* (Carlton TV/Bentley Productions), *Neanderthal's World* (Wall To Wall), *The Fast Show* (BBC Television), *Gulliver's Travels* (Jim Henson Productions), *Wall Of Silence* (Granada/LWT).
Radio includes: *Baghdad Wedding* (BBC Radio 3), *A Million Different People* (BBC Radio).

Sharona Sassoon **Aisha Khan**

Sharona was born in East London. She trained at Finch Stage School, Middlesex University and the New Paltz State University of New York, where she graduated with a BA in Performing Arts.

Sharona made her stage debut in *Bombay Dreams* (Really Useful Group/Victoria Apollo). Other Theatre credits include Cherry in *Where's My Desi Soulmate?* and Primilla in *The Deranged Marriage* (Rifco Arts), Sugary in the Olivier Nominated *Cinderella* (Theatre Royal, Statford East), *Many Voices* (TNT Theatre), *The Marriage of Figaro* and *An Enemy of the People* (Tara Arts), *Calcutta Kosher* and *Bells* (Kali Theatre Company), *27 Wagons Full of Cotton* (Black Box Theatre, New York), Mable in *Fame* (Gordon Craig Theatre) and *Blood on the Pavement* (Cockpit Theatre). Sharona is delighted to be working at The Theatre Royal once again!

Ruby Visaria **Jamillia Khan**

Television includes: *What's Your News?* (TT Animation); *Casualty* (BBC); *Eastenders*, (BBC); *England Expects* (BBC); *The Bill* (Pearson TV); *Londons Burning* (LWT); *Small Potatoes* (Hat Trick); *Wavelength* (Richmond Films).

Film includes: *Extraordinary Rendition* (Ultra Films) and *Hush Ya Mouth* (Greenwich Films). Theatre includes: *Handful of Henna* (The Crucible at Sheffield Theatres); *Katy Clay* and *2 Days as a Tiger* (New Vic Theatre).

Creative Team

Cosh Omar **Writer**

As a writer, Cosh's first play, *The Battle of Green Lanes*, launched the new Artistic Directorship of Kerry Michael at the Theatre Royal Stratford East and won the CEN Magazine award for best theatre. For Hampstead Theatre, 'Daring Pairing' writing festival, Cosh wrote *Thank God It's Friday* with Amy Rosenthal. Cosh's short story, *Son of a Hoca*, was one of the winning entries for The Decibel Penguin Prize and was published by Penguin in the anthology, *From There to Here*. Cosh's essay, *Rebel with a Cause: A Personal Journey from Sufism to Islamism and Beyond*, is to be published by Palgrave Macmillan in the book *The Other Muslims*, for the new year in the United States.

Kerry Michael **Director**

Kerry was appointed the Artistic Director and Chief Executive of Theatre Royal Stratford East in September 2004. Since then he has upheld the Theatre's commitment to develop new work and to provide a platform for those voices under-represented in the ever-changing communities of East London. Kerry's debut play as Artistic Director was *The Battle of Green Lanes* written by Cosh Omar – set amongst London's Cypriot community. In 2007 Theatre Royal was nominated for an Olivier Award for 'presenting a powerful season of provocative work that reaches new audiences'. Its hip-hop dance production, *Pied Piper* won an Olivier the same year. The following year, Kerry's production of *Cinderella* was nominated for an Olivier, the first pantomime nominated in the Award's history. Kerry's other Stratford East directing credits include numerous Christmas shows, various new plays including *Jamaica House* by Paul Sirett, which had a site specific performance on the top floor of a tower block in Stepney, new musicals *Make Some Noise* and *One Dance Will Do*. His most recent directing credits include *The Harder They Come,* which obtained wide critical acclaim transferring to the Barbican and the Playhouse Theatre in the West End before going on a very successful tour of Canada and the US; and Come Dancing which is set for a major UK tour in 2010. Kerry is a board member of Stratford Renaissance Partnership; a trustee of Discover, which provides creative, play and learning opportunities for children and their carers in Stratford; and a member of Equity's International Committee for Artists Freedom.

Yannis Thavoris Set & Costumes Designer

Yannis was born in Thessaloniki, Greece. He is the winner of the 1997 Linbury Prize for Stage Design. In 1995 he graduated from the School of Architecture at the Aristotle University of Thessaloniki and then studied at Central Saint Martin's College of Art & Design, where he graduated with a Master of Arts in 1997. Yannis has worked in opera, theatre and architecture. His recent designs include: *Petrushka* (Scottish Ballet at the 2009 Edinburgh Festival); *Katya Kabanova*, *Tosca*, *Jenufa* (Opera Holland Park); *Gigi* (Regent's Park Open Air Theatre); *Aïda* (sets – Welsh National Opera); *The Marriage of Figaro* (Sets – ENO); *Cosi Fan Tutte* (Sets – Opéra National du Rhin and Scottish Opera); *Annie Get Your Gun* (British tour); *La Clemenza di Tito* (Royal Danish Opera and ENO)
Work in progress includes two productions in the 2010 Opera Holland Park season. www.yannisthavoris.com

Prema Mehta Lighting Designer

Prema designs across the UK and Europe for drama, dance and opera productions. Drama designs include *The Electric Hills* (Liverpool Everyman), *Year 10* (Mettre en Scène, Rennes and Théâtre National de Strasbourg), *The Massacre* (Theatre Royal, Bury St Edmunds), *The House of Bernarda Alba* (Battersea Arts Centre), *Knock Against My Heart* (Unicorn Theatre). Dance designs include *Penguin Café* in collaboration with The London College of Fashion (Cochrane Theatre), *Ritual of Entrapment* (Purcell Room, South Bank Centre), *Trail* (National tour), *Spill* (semi-finals in The Place Prize) and *Parallels/ Dissonant/ Fine Line* (Lilian Baylis, Sadler's Wells). Opera and Musical designs include *The Puppini Sisters* (Bloomsbury Theatre), *Swingin' in Mid Dream* (Albany Theatre). Her work exhibited in the Collaborators exhibition at The Victoria and Albert Museum. www.premamehta.com

Theo Holloway Sound Designer

Theo's recent sound designs include: *Crossings* (Richmix and UK Tour), *Sign of the Times* (UK Tour), *A Plague Over England* (Duchess Theatre), *Pack of Lies* (UK Tour), *Cinderella* (Nottingham Theatre Royal), *Tons of Money* (UK Tour), *Cradle Me* (Finborough Theatre), *Make Me a Song* (New Players Theatre, Associate Sound Design), *I am a Superhero* (Theatre 503), *There's Something About Simmi* (Theatre Royal Stratford East and UK Tour), *The Vegemite* Tales (The Venue, Leicester Square). Theo works for Orbital Sound Limited, where he is also Head of Training, and the designated radio mic geek.

Matthew Blacklock **Assistant Director**

Matthew trained at East 15 Acting School. His previous directing experience includes *Anything Does Happen,* a promenade production that toured South London pubs for CROW Theatre; *Sleigh Bells Roasting* & *The Ad Man's New Year*, play readings at The RADA bar and *Operation New Life* that played at the Hen & Chickens, Inn on the Green & The Bedford for First Draft Theatre Co. He also collaborates on a monthly Live Art night at The Basement in Brighton called *The Basement Bordello* and regularly acts as host at Tea Dances for Ragroof Theatre. His last involvement with Theatre Royal was observing rehearsals on *The Battle of Green Lanes*.

Theatre Royal Stratford East Staff

Artistic Director	**Kerry Michael**
Executive Director	**Mary Caws**

Artistic
Associate Producer	**Karen Fisher**
Assistant to Artistic Director	**Rita Mishra**
Associate Artists	**Fred Carl (US), Robert Lee (US), Roger Robinson, Ryan Romain, Ultz, Matthew Xia**

Operations
General Manager	**Ali Fellows**
Theatre Manager	**Graeme Bright**
Operations Coordinator	**Velma Fontaine**
Resources/Technical Manager	**Stuart Saunders**
Head of Finance	**Paul Canova**
Finance Officers	**Elinor Jones and Titilayo Onanuga**
Projects Coordinator	**Emma Louise Norton**

Youth Arts & Education
Head of Youth Arts & Education	**Jan Sharkey-Dodds**
Project Manager	**Serena B. Robins**
Youth Arts Officer	**Karlos Coleman**

Marketing and Press
Head of Marketing & Sales	**Barry Burke**
Press & Marketing Officer	**Corinne O'Sullivan**
Marketing Officer	**Dan Parkington**
Box Office Manager	**Beryl Warner**
Box Office Supervisor	**Angela Frost**
Box Office Assistants	**Asha Bhatti, Ana Gizelda Burke, Kemisha Plummer, Yazmin Lacey-Phillips**

Archives
Theatre Archivist	**Murray Melvin**
Assistant Archivist	**Mary Ling**

Production
Head of Stage	**Simon Godfrey**
Chief Electrician	**David Karley**
Deputy Chief LX	**Kyle Macherson**
Wardrobe Manager	**Korinna Roeding**
Company & Stage Manager	**Sarah Buik**

Front of House

Senior Duty Manager	**Liz Okinda**
Duty Managers	**Nana Agyei, Jenine-Marie-Nelson, Danai Mavunga, Rameeka Parvez**
Head Ushers	**Alesha Ladeate-Williams, Sakaa Mensah**
Ushers	**Yemi Balogun, Rosie Christian, Tanoh Danso, Nicholas Fairclough-Underwood, Warren Humphrey, Thomas Jacob-Ewles, Joan Kugonza, Charles Leanson, Nikarika Mahandru, Doreen Ngozi Maina, Sade Olokodana, Benjamin Peters, Bradley Peters, Shereen Philips, Magda Sobckzanska, Sophie Tuitt, Heather Walker, Billy Walton, Andrew Wright**
Fire Marshalls	**Akosua Acheampong, Kofi Agyemang, Avita Jay, Charles Leanson, Catherine Philips**
Bar Supervisors	**Magdelena Molok**
Bar Team Leaders	**Ysanne Tidd, Terry Williams**
Bar Assistants	**Daniel Agudah, Jonathan Alagoa, Jamie Breck-Paterson, Desiree Brown, Agata Dziewiecka, Maia Gibbs, Daniel Morgan, Gemma Neve, Lydia Osych, Charlene Pierre, Rehema Nyange, Cregg St. Rose**
Domestic Assistants	**Julie Lee, Helen Mepham, Lynsey Webb, Magdalene Sobczynska**

Professional Advisors

Legal	**Neil Adleman at Harbottle & Lewis LLP**
Insurance	**Linda Potter at Giles Insurance Brokers**
Auditors	**Kingston Smith**
Development	**Sarah Mansell at SM Consultants**

Board of Directors

Sally Banks, Sarah Isted (*Treasurer*), **Jo Melville, Murray Melvin** (*Company Secretary*), **Paul O'Leary** (*Chair*), **Mark Pritchard, Jane Storie, Matthew Xia**

Please Support Theatre Royal

All this amazing work costs money and we need your help!

Theatre Royal Stratford East is a charity. Box office income and funding from our partners – Arts Council England, London Borough of Newham and London Councils – covers only **80% of our costs,** so every year we need to raise an additional **£250,000.**

Please will you consider supporting our inspirational programme for young people and the wider community or our work on stage, you could even commission a piece of new work. You could sponsor a production or youth project, make a donation or join our business club.

Every little bit helps.

Here are some of the ways you can help us

Make a donation towards our *Youth Arts Consortium* and support the work with young people; enabling them to explore the challenges they face, share their stories and uncover hidden talent and artists of the future.

Become a member of our *Vision Collective* and support emerging artists and new work. See our work 'from the inside' – benefits include a newsletter, invitations to briefings, rehearsals and workshops.

Join our *Business Club* and promote your business, entertain clients, reward and retain your staff. It is great fun and benefits include advertising, branding, business-2-business networking, hospitality, complimentary tickets and discounts.

Name a Seat and have a plaque with your inscription displayed on the seat.

Leave a legacy to the Joan Littlewood Fund and by leaving us a gift in your Will, you are ensuring that future generations will continue to enjoy the magic of Theatre Royal.

For further information on all Sponsorships, Donations, Memberships and Legacies, please contact Emma Louise Norton on **020 8279 1138** or **elnorton@stratfordeast.com**

We would like to thank the following for their support

With thanks to our funding partners:

Thanks to the support from the following Trusts and Foundations:

Causes Dear, Grange Park Opera, Heritage Lottery Fund, Jack Petchey Foundation, Joanie's Trust, London Metropolitan Police, Lord and Lady Lurgan Trust, Newham Summer Programme 2009, Paul Hamlyn Foundation, Youth Opportunity Fund.

The Vision Collective

With thanks to the ongoing support from our current Vision Collective members:

Sally Banks, Jim Broadbent, Derek Brown, Barbara Ferris, Mary Friel, Tony Hall, Elizabeth and Derek Joseph, Sofie Cooper Mason (*Offwestend.com*)**, Murray Melvin, Derek Paget, Jon Potts, SM Consultants, Vanessa Stone, Jane Storie, Geoff and Toni Sutton and Hedley G Wright – together with all those who wish to remain anonymous.**

We would like to thank the following businesses for their support: Arts Club, Clifford Chance LLP, Express by Holiday Inn London-Stratford, Goldline Cars, Harbottle & Lewis and Westfield Shopping Towns Limited.

We would also like to say thank you to the Avis Bunnage Estate and Richard Radcliffe for their support.

Birkbeck and Theatre Royal Stratford East

Birkbeck and Theatre Royal Stratford East believe that it is central to their aims and philosophy to play a leading role in the development of the cultural and social life of East London. Both organisations seek to offer a wide range of individuals the opportunity to develop their potential and enhance their lives, and are delighted to be working in partnership to deliver these outcomes. Birkbeck, University of London – London's specialist provider of part time evening university courses now in Stratford. Top qualifications from the University of London. Generous financial support and bursaries. For more information, visit www.birkbeckstratford.ac.uk.

Contacting the Theatre

Theatre Royal Stratford East
Gerry Raffles Square
Stratford
London
E15 1BN

e-mail **theatreroyal@stratfordeast.com**
Administration **020 8534 7374**
Fax **020 8534 8381**
Booking Line **020 8534 0310**
Box Office open **Mon – Sat 10am – 7pm**
We are delighted to take Typetalk calls
or if you prefer send us a text **07972 918 050**
Press Direct Line **020 8279 1120**

THEATRE ROYAL

$\mathcal{BAR}$

Free Entertainment 7 Days a Week

Open Daily: Mon-Thurs 10am-11pm, Fri 10am-12am,
Sat 11am-12am, Sun 12pm-11pm

Caribbean Flavours in the Theatre Royal Bar

The finest fish and chicken spiced and cooked to
perfection by our chef, Wills, as well as a wide range of
non-Caribbean food, salads and snacks.

Open daily: Mon 12:30pm-9:30pm, Tues & Weds
12:30pm-8:30pm, Thurs-Sat 12:30pm-9:30pm,
Sun 1pm-8pm

A Night Less Ordinary

Arts Council England in association with Metro brings
you the new scheme, A Night Less Ordinary. Launched
in February 2009 the scheme offers thousands of free
theatre tickets to anyone under 26 for all sorts of theatre
events including comedy, tragedies, musical theatre,
dance, modern mime, plays, circus and much more.

For more information log on to www.anightlessordinary.
org.uk

THE GREAT EXTENSION

First published in 2009 by Oberon Books Ltd
521 Caledonian Road, London N7 9RH
Tel: 020 7607 3637 / Fax: 020 7607 3629
e-mail: info@oberonbooks.com
www.oberonbooks.com

A catalogue record for this book is available from the British
Library.

ISBN: 978-1-84002-972-7

Cover design by Luke Wakeman

Printed in Great Britain by CPI Antony Rowe, Chippenham.

Characters

HASSAN

SANJAY

DAVID

MR BROWN

JAMILLIA

HAMID

ABDUL AZIZ

AISHA

MR HASSAN

MRS HASSAN

POLICEMAN

HANDSOME YOUNG TURKISH MAN

Act One

NEWS BULLETIN: The polite protocol between Nicolas
Sarkozy and Barack Obama proved short-lived after the
French President warned his US counterpart yesterday to
keep his nose out of the issue of Turkey's membership of
the European Union.

President Obama used his first EU/US summit, on the
eve of his visit to Turkey, to motivate European leaders to
embrace the Muslim country and 'anchor it in Europe'.

Mr Sarkozy, however, has been a long-standing opponent
of full membership for Turkey and brushed off the US
leader in language that seemed to upset the revival of
Franco-US relations.

Support for Turkey in joining the EU, a process it began
formally in 2005 and hopes to complete before 2020, has
long been an American foreign policy goal.

Mr Obama, who flew to Turkey overnight, obviously
wanted to leave on a positive note and told the EU leaders:
'The United States and Europe must approach Muslims as
our friends, neighbours and partners in fighting injustice,
intolerance and violence. Moving forward towards Turkish
membership in the EU would be an important signal
of your commitment to this agenda and ensure that we
continue to anchor Turkey......firmly in Europe.'

We hear the sound of a bustling building site.
The various tools slowly turn very rhythmic.
*After a few moments, the sound of Turkish Mevlana music with
heavy percussion is also heard. This adds greatly to the rhythmic
sound, which keeps building.*
*Now, from a distance, we hear the approach of the Mehter, the
Ottoman military band.*
*The sound of a man and woman having passionate sex is added to
the crescendo of throbbing hubbub.*

Lastly, we hear the builders break into a song:

'For he's a jolly good Hassan!
For he's a jolly good Hassan!
For he's a jolly good Haaassaaan!
Aaaaand...... Another one bites the dust!'

All sound ceases as we hear a roar of thunder and then rain.
Dim morning light comes through a skylight giving very little light
to the stage.
We hear someone crying in desperation.
Enter SANJAY.

SANJAY: Master?...... Master?...... Is that you?...... Oh, this is ridiculous... Why don't you put some lights on......

HASSAN: Don't you bloody dare... No lights!... No lights!

SANJAY: What's the matter?... Have you hurt yourself?

HASSAN: Hurt myself?... I've committed bloody suicide!

SANJAY: Oh, you poor thing............ I thought there was something wrong... I usually wake up to the sound of sex...... I look forward to that...... What's the matter?... Didn't she like the music?... She just might not be turned on by Sufi mysticism, that's all... Not everyone is, you know...... Unless, she was Islamophobic!... Was she?!... Bitch!!

HASSAN: No!!

SANJAY: Well, what is the fucking matter then?!... Look, I feel stupid talking in the dark... I only enjoy it with strangers and I've known you far too long.

HASSAN: No lights!... Please! No lights!

SANJAY: Oh, don't be so stupid.........

Lights up to reveal SANJAY by the light switch wearing a very camp
dressing gown and HASSAN in his black Armani suit curled up
under the baby grand piano looking very dishevelled and crying his
eyes out.

SANJAY is of Asian descent.
HASSAN is of Turkish descent.

...... Master?

On stage we see a very stylish split level home. Spread around we see a collection of antique furniture fashionably married with modern designer pieces. On the walls we see artwork that are a fusion of Sufi Islamic influence and contemporary abstract. There is also a very large abstract contemporary sculpture that is extremely erotic. This home is not family-oriented. It is extremely masculine and immaculately clean throughout.
Stage left there is a modern staircase that curls round a baby grand piano and leads to the upper floor. On the upper floor we see three doors leading to bedrooms and against the walls there are stylish bookshelves on which there is a large collection of expensively bound books. Looking up through a huge skylight window is a large antique telescope. It is pointed at the moon, which together with a star forms an abstract version of the Turkish flag.
On the lower level, stage right, there are big patio doors that are covered with plastic sheets which lead to the extension being built. The back wall is mostly of glass, through which we can see the silhouette of a crane and other apparatus from a building site.

HASSAN: Turn the light off!... Please... Turn the light off!

SANJAY: No, I won't... Come out from there... What are you hiding from?

HASSAN: I'm not coming out... I'm not coming out... Never!

SANJAY: Oh, shut up, you silly old tart!... What's the matter?... Did you have a bad dream?

HASSAN: The worst!... The worst!

SANJAY: Well, it's all over now.

HASSAN: But it's not!... It's not!

SANJAY: If that is some kind of comment on my gown then you can fuck off...... You bought me this in Paris.

HASSAN: Oh, Sanjay!… Sanjay!… Something very bad has happened.

SANJAY: Well, come out of there and tell me what it is.

HASSAN: No!… I'm not coming out!… I'm not coming out!

SANJAY: Look!… The bogeyman has gone… There's no one here but a very stylish and attractive camp Asian trannie…… Now, a butch Turkish man like you wouldn't be scared of me, now, would you?

HASSAN: You don't understand!

SANJAY: No!… I don't!…… Oh, look… I'm going to burn some olive leaves…maybe then you'll believe the bogeyman has gone.

SANJAY starts to move across the stage.

HASSAN: No!… Don't leave me!…
… Stay with me.

SANJAY: Who are you hiding from?

HASSAN: You really don't want to know.

SANJAY: Don't tell me you picked up a bit of rough trade last night?… My God!… She must be a right vixen if she was too rough for you… What did she do?… Tie you up and beat the shit out of you?

HASSAN: No!

SANJAY: A dominatrix who whipped you into a submissive sissy slut?

HASSAN: No!

SANJAY: Did she take control of your sexuality by bulldozing her way through all that testosterone only to unleash your inner sissy fag and fulfilled any naughty little submissive desires?

HASSAN: It's nothing like that!… Shut up!

SANJAY: Shame… I was getting excited there…… Well, whoever it is…she's struck terror into you……… I presume she's still here?

HASSAN: I think so.

SANJAY: Oh, you are cruel… Least you could do is give her a cup of tea… God knows what you've done to her.

HASSAN: Nothing!… I've done nothing to her…and no one can prove otherwise!

SANJAY: What is the matter with you?

HASSAN: You don't understand.

SANJAY: Well, I'm afraid, I don't…no.

HASSAN: Oh, Sanjay!

SANJAY: Oh, stop that!… Be a man!… Tell me what is wrong!

Pause.

HASSAN: This……erm……young lady……and……erm…… well, me……erm –

SANJAY: You and this young lady had passionate sex but the condom broke and now you both regret it… But, hey!… We all slip… and let's face it…you are a big boy.

HASSAN: No!

SANJAY: You did use a condom?

HASSAN: No!

SANJAY: You didn't use a condom!?

HASSAN: No!… It isn't that!

SANJAY: I've told you about that before… I don't want you anywhere near me if you don't use condoms with others… I mean, there's sexy fantasies and then there's death… And then no more sex or fantasies… I've got too much to live for, I tell yah!

HASSAN: It's nothing to do with that!... Shut the fuck up!

SANJAY: She's not dead, is she?

HASSAN: What?

SANJAY: Well, let's face it...you are a bit brutal... And real girls can't handle such savagery... I've told you that before. Oh my God!... You haven't fucked her to death, have you?

HASSAN: No!

SANJAY: I don't think I could handle a dead body in here... I mean, that's truly fucked, innit?

HASSAN: No!!... No! No! No!... I never touched her!... I swear it!... I never touched her and no one can prove otherwise!

SANJAY: Oh my God!... She's dead!

HASSAN: She's not fucking dead!... I didn't kill her or fuck her or anything!!

SANJAY: Anything?

HASSAN: Anything!

SANJAY: Nothing?

HASSAN: Nothing!

SANJAY: But if you didn't kill her...or fuck her...then what is it?!... What is the Problem?!!

Pause.

HASSAN: Me...and...this...young lady.........this young lady...and I......as in, us both...her and me...together –

SANJAY: What is it?!!!

HASSAN: We're.........married.

A roar of thunder.
Slight pause.

SANJAY: What did you say?

HASSAN: I said………we're………married.

A roar of thunder.

SANJAY: That's what I thought you said.

Slight pause.

SANJAY & HASSAN: Aaaaaaaaaaaaaaaaaaaaaaaaaaaaaaaaaaaaaaaa aaaaaaaa!!!!!!!!!!!!!!!!!!!!!!!!!!!!

SANJAY: What the hell happened?!… You went to your cousin's stag night not bloody yours!!… Did they mix the Hassans up or something!?… What the hell happened?!!!

HASSAN: I don't know!… I don't know!… I don't remember nothing!

SANJAY: Nothing!?… You get married and you don't remember nothing!?… You scatty old queen!!

HASSAN: All I have…is some vague memory of some kind of Mosque…and standing in front of some bloke with a big beard.

SANJAY: Jesus Christ!!

HASSAN: What am I going to do?!… What am I going to do?!!

SANJAY: Well, master… I don't know what you're going to do…you made your bed…and now you're going to have to lie in it…a designer four poster piece or not!… Me?!… I'm going to make 'an exit'.

SANJAY composes himself and then elegantly starts to ascend the stairs.

HASSAN: Sanjay!… Where are you going?!

SANJAY: To pack my things.

HASSAN: Sanjay!… You can't leave me!… Not now!

SANJAY: You have *her* now.

HASSAN: Her!... I don't even know who 'her' is!

SANJAY: Give it time.

HASSAN: Sanjay!... Please!... You can't leave me here with her!... Please!... I don't even know who she is!

SANJAY: 'She' is your wife.

HASSAN: No she's not!... Well, not really!... Oh, fuck!!... Sanjay, please don't leave me!!!

SANJAY: I'm sorry...but there can only be one queen bee in my space.

HASSAN: We'll get rid of her!!

SANJAY: How?

Suddenly, we hear the sound of the building site. The day's work on the extension has started.

HASSAN: We'll kill her!... We'll fucking kill her!... And bury her under the extension!

SANJAY: Well...it's a bit drastic.

Enter DAVID from the patio doors.
DAVID is in his hard-hat and builders gear except for his boots, which have been taken off and left by the patio doors.

HASSAN: Fuck!... Do you think he heard us?!

DAVID: Morning......... Everything OK?

HASSAN: No!!... Everything is not fucking OK!!

DAVID: I've come at a wrong time, haven't I?

HASSAN: Yes you have.

SANJAY: Not at all!... You can be the first to congratulate Master Hassan.

HASSAN: Shut up!

DAVID: Oh, really?... On what?

SANJAY: He's married.

DAVID: He's what?!

SANJAY: He's married.

DAVID: You're what!?

HASSAN: Oh, fucking hell!!

SANJAY: You'd be surprised at the things that end up back here when he's drunk... Of course, the next day he doesn't remember a thing.

HASSAN: It's not my fault...... I'm allergic to alcohol!

SANJAY: Acute episodic paroxysmal alcoholic amnesia.

HASSAN: Oh, yeah! Let the world know, why don't yah?!

SANJAY: A brain disorder, no less......the dozy cow.

DAVID: So why do you drink?

HASSAN: Well I forget, don't I!

DAVID & SANJAY: Of course.

SANJAY: You know...he's brought all kinds of things back here...but I never thought that it would one day be a wife.

DAVID: Drunk!?... Hold on, you're not suppose to be drinking... You're Muslim.

HASSAN: Oh, shut up, David!... Don't be so bloody naïve.

DAVID: Well...congratulations.

HASSAN: Congratulations?!

DAVID: On being married.

HASSAN: Oh, piss off!

DAVID: Well, where is she then?

HASSAN: Who?

DAVID: Your wife.

HASSAN: Don't call her that!

DAVID: Where is she?

SANJAY: Yeah… Where is she?… This one I'd like to meet.

HASSAN: I'm not sure…but I think……she's up……there.

All three stare up to the bedroom doors.

SANJAY: Right… It's time we meet, Mrs Hassan.

SANJAY starts to make his way up the stairs towards the bedroom.

HASSAN: Don't you fucking dare!

SANJAY: We'll have to meet her at some point.

HASSAN: Don't you fucking dare call her Mrs Hassan!

SANJAY: Well, going by what you're saying…she is!

DAVID: Don't you remember anything?

SANJAY: All he has…is a vague memory of some kind of Mosque…and standing in front of some bloke with a big beard.

DAVID: Jesus Christ!

HASSAN: Oh, my God!

DAVID: Listen, it happens to the best of us.

HASSAN: Ah, but it doesn't!

SANJAY: It did!

HASSAN: Oh, bloody hell!

DAVID: It's not that bad… I've been married for sixteen years.

HASSAN: You haven't?

DAVID: I have.

HASSAN: That's disgusting!

DAVID: Oi!

HASSAN: That's just so bloody –

SANJAY: Last century –

HASSAN: So fucking last century.

DAVID: It's not that bad, I tell yah.

HASSAN: Not that bad!?… Marriage, my son…is a painful death that slowly eats away at your character, killing everything that makes you 'you'…until there's nothing left of 'you'…till all you are is one big mass of compromise.

DAVID: Now, hold on –

HASSAN: Oh here we go, Sanjay… The pacified man defending his institutionalisation.

SANJAY: Well, you'd know.

DAVID: Pacified man!?

HASSAN: Yes!… Pacified man!… I mean tell me if I'm wrong… When you first got together you desperately tried to impress her by showing her what a man you are…therefore being a right male chauvinist pig… Which of course fell very uncomfortable with her –

DAVID: Well, kind of –

HASSAN: Then, of course, you two started having troubles…at which point you shat your pants at the thought of losing her… So, you started to look for the middle ground… somewhere where you still felt like a man but where you felt you were making concessions… I mean, how bloody nice of you!… And it worked, things got a lot better… You were getting on again!… Finding the middle ground led to conciliation…the future looked nothing but rosy, you were in love… Then before you knew it, your conciliation through finding 'the middle ground' lead to her wanting more negotiation…more 'give and take'…which inevitably led to more trouble which led back to reconciliation through more negotiation which inevitably lead to nothing but fucking pacification!...... Henceforth, you have the pacified man.

DAVID: I wish I never came in here... I'm getting very depressed.

HASSAN: Well...you made your bed...... It's not our fault that it's not a designer four poster piece that sees lots of action like –

SANJAY: Like ours?... I don't think so... It's hers now...all ready to pacify you in.

HASSAN: Shut up!

DAVID: Can I just get my tea please?

HASSAN: Of course... Sanjay, get David a cup of tea.

SANJAY: Yes, Master.

HASSAN: I mean look at my poor bastard cousin, Hassan, whose stag night it was –

DAVID: Your cousin, 'Hassan'?

HASSAN: That's right.

DAVID: But your name is 'Hassan'.

HASSAN: I know it is.

DAVID: And your family name is, 'Hassan'.

HASSAN: And?

DAVID: 'Hassan Hassan'?

SANJAY: He's so good they named him twice...... And who's the bitch that's cornered him?

HASSAN: My uncle's daughter.

DAVID: Your cousin?!

HASSAN: Yeah.

THE GREAT EXTENSION: ACT ONE

SANJAY: Which uncle?

HASSAN: My uncle, Hassan.

DAVID: So, hold on…… Hassan…that is, Hassan Hassan… cousin of Hassan Hassan…is marrying uncle Hassan's daughter…his first cousin.

HASSAN: Yeah.

SANJAY: This bit you'll love… What's her name?

HASSAN: Sandra.

DAVID: Sandra?!

HASSAN: Well, uncle Hassan's married to an English woman……… Which didn't go down too well in the family when it happened…as you can imagine……but my uncle was never into religion and that……so much so that when he had a boy, he didn't even bother circumcising him…… which wasn't too clever… Last year when that boy, my cousin married our other cousin…my aunty, knowing her brother, asked if his son was circumcised…… When he, she found out he wasn't she made him get it done……at the age of twenty-four.

DAVID: Bloody hell!!

HASSAN: Yeah, I really felt for Junior…not as much as he felt it though, I'm sure.

DAVID: Junior?

HASSAN: Yeah… My uncle and his wife came to an arrangement… They said they'd name the girl an English name…which is fair enough…but that the boy…following an English tradition… would be named after the father.

DAVID: Hassan?!

SANJAY: Yep.

HASSAN: You see what I mean?… You get married and everything gets cluttered up… My family don't even know their Hassans from their Hassans anymore............ Well, that's not this Hassan's problem –

SANJAY: No?

HASSAN: My cousin's made his bed and now he'll have to lie in it.

DAVID: And I bet it won't be no designer four poster piece that sees lots of action, either.

HASSAN: No it bloody won't, mate......... One year from now when there's nothing but the stink of dirty nappies everywhere and they don't get a wink of sleep because little baby Hassan has kept them up all night, they won't give a monkey's what the bed looks like... When his perfectly gym-toned body has gone to pot from all the lazy cooking that they have to munch through they'll forget what that bed was for altogether... And then one day he'll wake up and find that he's such a fat compromised piece of shit that she's gone and fucking left him for something better...and let's face it...who can blame her, hey?

DAVID: Bloody hell.

HASSAN: I'm sorry, David...but if there was other any married men listening right now...they'd agree with me...trust me, they would...... I mean, look around you... No clutter... I like to keep my space and mind clear... Come on, Sanjay, where's his bloody water?!

SANJAY: Sorry, Master...it's on its way.

HASSAN: But most of all... I like to keep my space and mind... mine! All bloody mine!... No bloody pretences...no pretending to be something that I'm not... I like to know what I am and bloody stick to it!......

DAVID: What is that?!

HASSAN has suddenly noticed the large abstract contemporary sculpture that is extremely erotic.

SANJAY: He brought that back from some auction… He was very drunk.

DAVID: Blimey!…… You really shouldn't drink, you know.

HASSAN: It's bloody, Armani, innit!

SANJAY: Ooh, I doubt if it's one of his.

HASSAN: This bloody suit!… The last time I wore this suit was at my grandfather's funeral…… Now I go and wear it to my cousin's stag night… From mourning the loss of one Hassan……to another…… I should have known it would be a lethal blend… Armani and the Peckham Hassans.

DAVID: The 'Peckham' Hassans?

SANJAY: Yes… Distant relatives along the evolution line from the Kensington Boltons.

DAVID: There seems to be a lot of Hassans about these days.

HASSAN: The world is getting smaller, my son…we were always there…it's just the world is getting smaller…… I'm gonna burn it with olive leaves.

SANJAY: What?

HASSAN: This Armani suit.

Suddenly, we hear an electronic chime of 'Jerusalem' by William Blake.

HASSAN: Who could that be?… God, I hate people popping round willy-nilly.

DAVID: It might be another Hassan.

HASSAN: Don't be silly… There's not a Hassan left in the streets… They're all at home nursing their hangovers… Anyway, they'd know better than to just turn up… I wouldn't have 'em…cluttering up the place.

SANJAY: I'll see who it is.

HASSAN: Hold on!… What about her?

DAVID: It's that neighbour of yours, Mr Brown, I'd put money on it… That's what I came in to tell you about.

HASSAN: Oh, don't worry about him… He's just a bloody busybody.

DAVID: I know!… He's out every day with his measuring tape…checking every bloody thing we do.

HASSAN: David, my son…don't worry about a thing… This is my bloody land and I'll do what I bloody want with it.

DAVID: Oh, but I do worry…every time I see him with that tape measure.

HASSAN: Well…that's your problem, David, my son…you worry too much.

SANJAY: You know why?… He's married.

HASSAN: Fuck!… Right… Sanjay answer the door –

SANJAY: Yes, master.

SANJAY exits.

HASSAN: But what ever you do, don't let him in…… No one is allowed in until I sort this shit out.

Offstage we hear MR BROWN and SANJAY.

MR BROWN'S VOICE: Oh, my God!… What are you wearing, boy?!…… Look, I know he's home and I want to talk to him.

SANJAY'S VOICE: But he's busy.

MR BROWN'S VOICE: Busy!… Doing what?

DAVID: Oh, bloody hell…it is Mr Brown!

DAVID panics and tries to make a quick exit.

Enter MR BROWN holding a measuring tape and land deeds, quickly followed by SANJAY.
MR BROWN is a retired Englishman.

MR BROWN: Mr Hassan!… Do you have to let him answer the front door looking like that?!

HASSAN: Mr Brown………… You haven't taken your shoes off…… Sanjay!… Mr Brown hasn't taken his shoes off.

SANJAY: He just shot in here.

MR BROWN: What is this…a bloody Mosque?!

HASSAN: No, Mr Brown…we just like to keep the place nice and tidy.

MR BROWN: Yeah…well you could have fooled me… It might as well be a Mosque…the bloody sounds I hear coming out…either that or a bloody whorehouse…… You don't hear that from my house, do you, Mr Hassan?

HASSAN: No you don't, Mr Brown.

DAVID is trying very hard to sneak out without being noticed by MR BROWN.

MR BROWN: Mr Hassan?

HASSAN: Yes, Mr Brown?

MR BROWN: You can tell 'Bob the Builder' there, that I've already clocked him…so there's no point of him sneaking off.

HASSAN: David!

DAVID: Mr Hassan?

HASSAN: Mr Brown.

DAVID: Hello, Mr Brown.

MR BROWN: Hello…… 'Bob'.

DAVID: It's 'David'… Mr Brown.

MR BROWN walks over to the artwork on the wall.

MR BROWN: What's all this crap, then, hey?

HASSAN: It's art, Mr Brown.

MR BROWN: It looks 'Islamic' to me... Mr Hassan!

HASSAN: 'Islamic' art, Mr Brown.

MR BROWN: No such bloody thing... Mr Hassan!

SANJAY: Oh!... He's an art critic... I always wondered what he was.

MR BROWN: I might not know as much about art as your kind...Marigold!... But I know that *that*...is not art......it's 'Islamic'!...... And what the bloody hell is that?!

MR BROWN has just noticed the very large abstract contemporary sculpture that is extremely erotic.

HASSAN: It's more art, Mr Brown.

MR BROWN: Is it?

HASSAN: I think so.

MR BROWN: It looks more like perverted crap to me.

HASSAN: You might be right.

MR BROWN: Well, I won't pretend otherwise, Mr Hassan... Your type make me feel very uneasy.

HASSAN: My type, Mr Brown?

MR BROWN: Yes, Mr Hassan...your type...... Islamists... I mean, you might pass yourselves off as modern...and try and look all European...but deep down let's face it...you're all one big terrorist cell waiting to blow up!

HASSAN: Well, I must rush, Mr Brown... I'm going to an unveiling of a statue at the Bin Laden Appreciation Society and I can't be late... I'm pulling the cord.

MR BROWN: Ha bloody ha. I mean...you come over and do nothing but sponge off our government and then you want to blow up the place.

HASSAN: That reminds me…did I sign on at the DSS this week, Sanjay?

SANJAY: I don't think you did, master… We'll have to call them later.

HASSAN: You call them, Sanjay… I'm afraid I'm at the training camp later… Hope you've washed my camouflaged balaclava.

SANJAY: Washed and pressed, master…not a drop of blood in sight.

MR BROWN: You wait, Hassan! –

HASSAN: 'Mr' Hassan!… Mr Brown.

MR BROWN: 'Mr' Hassan, you might be single now but once you get married –

HASSAN: Mr Brown!… Now you go too far!

SANJAY: We don't allow such language in this house.

HASSAN: No we fucking don't!

MR BROWN: Once you get married –

HASSAN: Never!

SANJAY: Never?

HASSAN: 'Never', I say!

MR BROWN: And have children! –

HASSAN: Stop it!… It burns!… It burns!

MR BROWN: Then you'll show your real self…and I will be stuck with a bunch of covered up Islamists living next door to me!

HASSAN: You can be so cruel!!

MR BROWN: Which brings me to my point…… Your extension!… Apart from having to listen to all that racket that those Turkish builders make...half the time I don't understand what they're bloody saying –

DAVID: My workers aren't Turkish!

MR BROWN: No!?... Well, what the bloody hell are they, then?!

DAVID: Polish.

HASSAN: Ah, well!... That's not so bad, then...is it, Mr Brown?

MR BROWN: Well...not so bad......still bloody foreigners, though...... Anyway!... That land between me and you... is still disputed land......and we both know that it's mine –

HASSAN: Well, not really, Mr Brown...that's why it's 'disputed'... But I think you'll find that it is mine to build on.

MR BROWN: I'm watching you, Hassan!

HASSAN: 'Mr' Hassan.

MR BROWN: 'Mr' Hassan!... These deeds that I hold will prove that it is my land... But until it's all sorted out...you can only extend to the undisputed line!... No more!

HASSAN: Mr Brown!... I promise you...that until I get permission... I will only build to the undisputed line... But once I get my permission...you and I will be as snug...as a bug......in a Turkish rug.

MR BROWN: Bloody hell!

HASSAN: Now, I really must rush, Mr Brown.

Slight pause.

MR BROWN: Mr Hassan.

HASSAN: Mr Brown.

Exit MR BROWN.

DAVID: What a nasty piece of work.

SANJAY: There seems to be more and more of them these days.

HASSAN: Don't be silly… The world is getting smaller…… They were always there……it's just the world is getting smaller……… I'm so knackered… I think I'll go to bed and sleep.

SANJAY: Go to bed and sleep?!… Don't you think you've forgotten something?

HASSAN: Oh, bloody hell!

> *Pause.*
> *HASSAN, SANJAY and DAVID all stand still and stare up to the bedroom doors.*
> *Then, slowly and timidly, HASSAN and SANJAY begin to ascend the stairs.*

DAVID: I wonder what she's doing?

HASSAN: I don't care.

SANJAY: Yes you do.

HASSAN: No I don't.

SANJAY: You should… She could be doing anything up there.

HASSAN: Fucking hell.

DAVID: You'll have to speak to her at some point.

HASSAN: Why?

DAVID: Well, what's her name?

HASSAN: Who gives a shit?

DAVID: What does she look like?

HASSAN: I don't fucking remember.

> *Enter JAMILLIA, stepping out from behind the sculpture.*

JAMILLIA is wearing a long black coat and a black scarf around her head.
JAMILLIA is of Pakistani descent.

DAVID: You don't remember?

HASSAN: I don't remember, I tell yah.

Suddenly, SANJAY notices JAMILLIA.

SANJAY: Oh!...... Hello, love.

HASSAN: Hello.

SANJAY: Not you, you dozy cow!... Her...... Your wife, I presume.

Both HASSAN and DAVID slowly turn their heads to see who SANJAY is talking about.
Pause.

Well, I must say, this is different.........

HASSAN breaks down in tears again. Slight pause.

...... This isn't a new fetish we've got, is it?

HASSAN: No it bloody isn't!

Pause.

SANJAY: So!... What's your name then?

HASSAN: No!!... We don't want to know her name...... We don't want to know anything about her.

DAVID: Oh, you are cruel... Least you could do is ask her her name.

SANJAY: God knows what you've done to her.

HASSAN: Nothing!... I've done nothing to her...and no one can prove otherwise!

DAVID: Hello.

HASSAN: Don't 'hello' her!... We were trying to work out how to get rid of her!!

DAVID: Get rid of her?

HASSAN: Yes!!

DAVID: Well......why d'you marry her?

HASSAN: I don't remember!!

DAVID: Poor girl.

HASSAN: Poor bloody girl!?

DAVID: Well...look at her...... I mean, I'm only guessing here...but she's not your usual type, is she?

HASSAN: No she bloody isn't!

SANJAY: No!... Usually, it's some high heeled tart that he seduces with Sufi mystic music...... Once he's got rid of her and we're back to the same old mediocre jazz...... then I know she's gone... Oh, yeah...he's a pretentious bastard...but he's very good at it.

HASSAN: There was no Sufi mystic music!

DAVID: And I hear no mediocre jazz.

SANJAY: And she ain't gone.

DAVID: Poor thing.

SANJAY: She does look like fish out of water.

DAVID: She's probably never been to some strange bloke's home before.

SANJAY: Well...technically speaking...he's not some strange bloke...he's her husband...... Poor thing.

HASSAN: Shut up!... Shut up!... I'm not her husband!

SANJAY: I think you are... You said you are.

DAVID: Poor girl.

HASSAN: Shut up!!… One minute we're talking about getting rid of her –

SANJAY: Burying her under the extension if I remember correctly –

HASSAN: And then you come in…and it's all 'poor thing' this and 'poor girl' that!… What about me, hey?!… What about me?!!

DAVID: Getting rid of her?!… Burying her under the extension?!… She's Muslim not bloody deaf!… She's hearing everything you're saying.

Pause. All three men become painfully aware of JAMILLIA's presence.

SANJAY: We should ask her name or something.

HASSAN: I don't want to know her name… I don't want to know anything about her.

Slight pause.

DAVID: Well, I think it's safe to say…that she's religious.

SANJAY: From a religious family.

DAVID: With a religious upbringing.

SANJAY: No contact with boys……until last night that is.

HASSAN: Oh, fucking hell!!

SANJAY: And you can stop that kind of language from now.

Slight pause.

DAVID: Her family must be going crazy thinking where she is.

SANJAY: I bet she's never had a single night away from them.

Slight pause.

DAVID, SANJAY & HASSAN: Bloody hell!!

HASSAN: What have I done?!… What have I done?!…
    Poor girl.

DAVID: You're going to have to contact her family.

HASSAN: What?!… No fucking way!!

DAVID: You're going to have to.

SANJAY: You married their daughter.

HASSAN: I'm not contacting no one!

SANJAY: And the Hassans… You'll have to tell them too.

HASSAN: You're having a laugh!!

SANJAY: Well, maybe not all of them…but your parents…
    you'll have to.

HASSAN: Fuck off!!

DAVID & SANJAY: Language!!

HASSAN: I'm sorry!… I'm so bloody sorry!… I need a drink.

DAVID: That's how you got into this trouble in the first place.

SANJAY: And anyway…you can't drink in front of her.

DAVID: There's a lot of things you won't be able to do in front
    of her.

SANJAY: That's true.

HASSAN: Listen!… This is my bloody home and I'll do what I
    bloody want!……

    *Suddenly, we hear the electronic chime of 'Jerusalem' by William
    Blake.*

    …… Oh, bloody hell!

DAVID: It's the front door.

HASSAN: I know it's the bloody front door!!… It's *my* bloody
    front door!!……… Sanjay?

After a slight pause SANJAY calmly walks down the stairs and exits to see who is at the front door.

MR BROWN'S VOICE: Oh, my God!… You not changed yet, marigold?!……

Enter MR BROWN holding the land deeds and quickly followed by SANJAY.

…… Mr Hassan!…

MR BROWN is suddenly confronted with the vision of JAMILLIA.

… What the bloody hell is that?!!

Slight pause.

HASSAN: It's a woman, Mr Brown.

MR BROWN: Looks 'Islamic' to me!

HASSAN: An 'Islamic' woman, Mr Brown!

MR BROWN: How can you tell?

HASSAN: Trust me!

MR BROWN: Trust you!?… Never.

SANJAY: Mr Brown……meet… Mrs Hassan.

MR BROWN & HASSAN: Mrs Hassan!?

HASSAN: Shut up, Sanjay!

SANJAY: Yes… Mrs Hassan… Mr Hassan's Mrs.

MR BROWN: Jesus Christ!!… I know I said it would happen!… But I only said it 20 minutes ago!!

SANJAY: I know!… Believe me, it was a surprise to us all.

MR BROWN: I mean!… I knew it would happen!… But not this bloody quick!… I mean, where did you get her from?!… Did you have her faxed over from Turkey via 'dial a bride'?!… There aren't anymore coming is there?!

SANJAY: No… No……… It all happened last night apparently.

MR BROWN: Last night?!

DAVID: In a Mosque… In front of a bloke with a big beard.

MR BROWN: Jesus Christ!!

SANJAY: I know…we're all in shock.

MR BROWN: You're in shock?!… Bloody hell!… You lot move fast, I tell yah!… I knew it would happen but bloody hell!!… Turn my back and you're already multiplying.

HASSAN: Yes, Mr Brown…can you get to the point!

MR BROWN: Well… I won't ask if I can kiss the bride!… But does she have a name?!… Does she speak English?!

SANJAY: We're not quite sure.

MR BROWN: Not quite bloody sure?!… What kind of people are you?!… Didn't you have time to ask?!

HASSAN: Not yet, no!

MR BROWN: My God!

HASSAN: Now!… What can I do for you, Mr Brown?!

MR BROWN: She don't say much, does she?

HASSAN: No!… I cut her tongue out to save me hassle!

MR BROWN: He hasn't has he?

HASSAN: It's an Islamic tradition…our foreskins, their tongues…it works out just fine!

MR BROWN: My God!

HASSAN: It's not too bad… If they prove to be good wives… we sew the tongue back on… I mean they're the lucky ones really…our foreskins got chucked away years ago!

MR BROWN: It's barbaric!

HASSAN: No!!…'Islamic'!!

MR BROWN realises that he's being had as SANJAY and DAVID can't contain their laughter.

MR BROWN: Oh, very funny…very funny! If I had any sense I'd knock your block off.

HASSAN: Well, it's a good job for me that you don't have any sense.

MR BROWN & HASSAN: Yes it is, mate…yes it is.

DAVID: Here…don't she have to pray or something?

HASSAN & MR BROWN: Pray?!

MR BROWN: That's all I need… Islamic praying going on next door to me.

SANJAY: Five times a day.

HASSAN: What?!

SANJAY: I've got a prayer-mat upstairs…do you remember, we bought it in Egypt… I'll bring it down.

HASSAN: I'm not having that thing down here!

DAVID: Why not?

SANJAY: It will mess his colour system up.

HASSAN: Yes it bloody will!

DAVID: Which way is east, anyway?

HASSAN: What?

SANJAY: She has to pray towards the east.

DAVID: Towards Mecca.

MR BROWN: There use to be a Mecca down Tottenham…that's not east…it's north.

DAVID: Not the gambling establishment… Mecca in Saudi Arabia.

MR BROWN: I'm only bloody joking!… My God!… We're still aloud to joke in this country, you know… Your draconian 'anti-hate' laws hasn't stopped that yet.

SANJAY: I think they have.

MR BROWN: Have they?!

HASSAN: Yep.

MR BROWN: Shit!!

SANJAY: I'll get the prayer mat.

MR BROWN: You can't let her pray!… I won't have it!

HASSAN: You won't have it!?

MR BROWN: Listen!… All that crap you believe in is in those prayers, innit!… All that mumbling of your bigoted crap –

SANJAY: Oh, that's bloody fresh.

MR BROWN: Listen… I've read the Koran.

SANJAY: Oh, you read Arabic, do yah?

MR BROWN: No I bloody don't read Arabic… I've read bits of translations.

SANJAY: 'Bits' of translations?

MR BROWN: Yes!… Bits of translations!… You don't have to read the whole bloody thing just to get the gist of it, do yah!?… I mean when they pray they quote passages from the Koran…and passage after passage they're warned against taking unbelievers as friends…that the unbelievers are their enemies –

DAVID: And there was you being a real chum.

MR BROWN: Listen, Bob!… Whose side are you on?

DAVID: Not yours… And it's 'David'!

MR BROWN: I'm only saying this because the Koran tells them that they should make war on the infidels… That's us!… The bloody infidels!

HASSAN: You know, I never realised you were such a scholar on Islam, Mr Brown.

MR BROWN: Oh and I suppose our leaders are when they tell us Islam is a peace loving religion… I mean…where are we going, hey?!… It's the death of a civilisation!… Through so-called multiculturalism and political correctness that completely prevents us from having any control on the bloody intolerant minority which at the end of the day sees its expansion and domination as its religious bloody duty!!

HASSAN: Mr Brown…you're going red in the face.

DAVID: You want to see him from this angle…he's got a big blue vein throbbing away on the back of his neck.

HASSAN: You really want to take it easy, Mr Brown.

SANJAY: Poor love.

HASSAN: Silly question…but why's he got his shoes in a bag?

MR BROWN: I mean, think about it… When we wanted to get rid of Saddam Hussein…you 'British' Muslims said, 'Oh we're not behind him…him and his government are un-Islamic'!… Well if *they're* un-Islamic…what the fuck are *we*?!

MR BROWN is bright red in the face and gasping for breath. HASSAN, DAVID and SANJAY gather to abet him.

HASSAN: Mr Brown!

SANJAY: Oh, the poor thing!

DAVID: You've really got to calm down, mate.

HASSAN: A glass of water for Mr Brown, Sanjay.

SANJAY: Of course.

SANJAY gets MR BROWN a glass of water.

MR BROWN: I only came to tell you that I've got in touch with my solicitor…and that he's trying to rush the council into making a decision…over whose land it is between us… Not that it's bloody worth anything now!

MR BROWN is banging the deeds against his head.

HASSAN: You relax, Mr Brown.

MR BROWN: They should be coming to a decision soon… They will be contacting us both.

HASSAN: Well, thank you, Mr Brown… You've told me now… But you've really got to calm down.

MR BROWN: I know…my doctor says the same thing to me…but I can't help it… I worry!

HASSAN: I know… I know.

SANJAY: I think you should go home and have a lie down.

DAVID: Get your mind off it all.

MR BROWN: I think you're right………

MR BROWN begins to be carefully escorted out by the others.

…… I'm watching you, Hassan.

HASSAN: 'Mr' Hassan… Mr Brown.

MR BROWN: Jesus Christ.

HASSAN: I know… I know.

Exit MR BROWN, HASSAN, SANJAY and DAVID.
JAMILLIA is left on stage on her own.
Slight pause.
Enter HASSAN, SANJAY and DAVID.

HASSAN: You know… I think I'll have a lie down after all that… I might even have a hot cocoa, please, Sanjay.

HASSAN starts to head up the stairs.

SANJAY: Oh, the poor brain-dead bitch...... It's all part of his paroxysmal alcoholic amnesia......complete apathy......no sense of urgency. Master?...... Haven't you forgotten something?

All three men's attention turns to JAMILLIA.

HASSAN: Bloody hell!

Long pause.

DAVID: Are you OK?

HASSAN: Oi!... She's my wife!

DAVID: Okay!

SANJAY: Your what?

HASSAN: You know what I mean.

SANJAY: You're getting a bit possessive!

HASSAN: I'm not getting possessive!

SANJAY: Well, you sound a bit keen to me.

HASSAN: Oh, shut up, Sanjay!... I just think I'm the one who should be asking the questions.

SANJAY: Well, go on then, ask!...... You just sound a bit keen, that's all.

HASSAN: Oh, shut up, you tart!!

SANJAY: Bitch!

Long pause. HASSAN is nervous.

HASSAN: Hello.

SANJAY: Hello?!... Is that it?!... Not Shakespeare, not Marlowe, not Blake......but Lionel bloody Ritchie!... Hello!

HASSAN: Will you shut up!!!......

Pause.

...... What's...... What's your name?

Slight pause.

JAMILLIA: Jamillia.

Slight pause.

HASSAN: Jamillia!... Oh...that's pretty.

DAVID: It is, yes...very pretty.

HASSAN: It is!... Very pretty...... Jamillia.

SANJAY: (*Mockingly.*) *Oh, that's so pretty... Really pretty that is......*
You married her last night!... You must have heard her
fucking name before!

HASSAN: Language!

Slight pause.

Do you......speak English?

SANJAY: Of course she speaks English!... How do you think
she understood the first question!

HASSAN: I'm gonna bitch-slap you in a minute... I swear to
fucking God, I am!!

SANJAY: It'll be a first.

DAVID: Guys!... Guys!... Language, please!

HASSAN: You can shut up as well......... Jamillia......
You see...... I think this whole thing......has been a
mistake......and it's not your fault –

SANJAY: No!... You weren't to know you were marrying an
amnesic drunk.

HASSAN: You see... I do some really stupid things when I
drink...... I mean, admittedly, never as stupid as this......

but......see...the next day I... I...never remember...and... well...... I'm very sorry... I can see that this don't usually happen to you either –

SANJAY: Oh, yeah...every day.

HASSAN: What I mean to say is......you obviously...... don't.........drink......or...anything.

SANJAY: What he's trying to say is...it's obvious that you're a nice girl.

HASSAN: Yeah...that's it......a nice girl............... It really is a pretty name.

DAVID: Very pretty.

SANJAY: Not that bloody pretty!

HASSAN: Well......you see......we'll have to sort all this out......don't worry......we'll, erm –

SANJAY: Call your family.

HASSAN: We're not going to call her family!

SANJAY: And the Hassans.

HASSAN: You can forget it!... I'm not calling the bloody Hassans!

SANJAY: We'll see.

HASSAN: Anyway, we'll all sit down......and put an end to this...fiasco.

JAMILLIA: An end?

Slight pause.

HASSAN: Well –

SANJAY: Yes!... An end.

HASSAN: Well…you see……it would never work…between someone like me and you…… I mean……you're such a……nice girl –

DAVID: Very nice.

HASSAN: And I'm………well –

SANJAY: A nasty piece of shit!

Slight pause.

HASSAN: It is a pretty name.

DAVID: Very.

SANJAY: Master!

HASSAN: Well, anyway……what I'm trying to say…is…… I'm not really the marrying kind.

SANJAY: No you're bloody not!

HASSAN: And anyway………you wouldn't want someone like me.

JAMILLIA: No?

SANJAY: No!

HASSAN: Fuck, I need a drink!

DAVID: Language!

HASSAN: Oh, shut up!…

A mobile phone starts ringing. The ringtone is 'Like a Virgin', by Madonna.

… Bloody hell, where's my phone?

SANJAY: That's not your phone.

DAVID: Well, it's not mine…… Is it yours?

SANJAY: 'Like a Virgin'?… Please!

JAMILLIA pulls out a mobile phone and answers it.

HASSAN: My God!… That's weird!

DAVID: What?

HASSAN: She's got a mobile phone.

JAMILLIA: (*Finishing her quick telephone call.*) Can I use your bathroom please?

HASSAN: Hey?

JAMILLIA: A bathroom?

SANJAY: Of course, dear… Up the stairs…and it's the last door…… It's the guest room and it's ensuite… There's fresh towels in the cupboard.

JAMILLIA starts to make her way up the stairs.

DAVID: See!… She has to do her ablution before praying.

HASSAN: Her what?

SANJAY: I'll come and put the prayer mat out for you, shall I?

JAMILLIA: Excuse me?

SANJAY: You need to pray, right?

JAMILLIA: Praying might help.

SANJAY also makes his way up the stairs and goes through the last door along the corridor with JAMILLIA.

HASSAN: Blimey!… Is that how it works, then?

DAVID: What?

HASSAN: They get a phone call every time they have to pray?

DAVID: No!… Well?… Maybe?

HASSAN: And who makes the calls?

Both HASSAN and DAVID slowly look up to the gods.
Suddenly, they are both startled by the electronic chime of 'Jerusalem' by William Blake.

HASSAN & DAVID: Jesus Christ!

SANJAY comes rushing out of the guest room.
As he does, we hear the sound of a shower.

SANJAY: There's somebody at the front door.

HASSAN: No! Really?… It's that bloody Mr Brown!

SANJAY: Oh, I wish it was!

HASSAN: What're you on about?

SANJAY: It's her family!

HASSAN: Whose family?!

SANJAY: Hers!!

DAVID: How can you tell?

SANJAY: Well, they don't look like no Jehovah's Witnesses!…
    She must have phoned them!

HASSAN: What?!… Well, ask her!

SANJAY: She's in the bathroom.

DAVID: Doing her ablution.

HASSAN: Oh, shut up!… Right!!… Well, I ain't seeing them!!

HASSAN runs up the stairs.

SANJAY: You have to!

HASSAN: No I don't!… I don't have to do a bloody thing!…
    Acute episodic paroxysmal alcoholic amnesia… Forgotten
    all about it already!

HASSAN disappears into a bedroom.
SANJAY looks at DAVID.

DAVID: Don't look at me!… I'm just the bloody builder!

SANJAY: At times like this we have to stick together……

Again, we hear the chime of 'Jerusalem' by William Blake.

... I need your help!

DAVID: Bloody hell!

SANJAY: You let them in and I'll be down in a minute.

DAVID: What!?

SANJAY: Well, look at me... We don't want the first thing they see to be me like this, now do we?

DAVID: I think you look rather nice.

SANJAY: Why, thank you!... Now open the bloody door!

SANJAY disappears into a bedroom.
DAVID is left alone.
Nervously, he inches off stage to answer the front door.
Enter JAMILLIA's brother, ABDUL AZIZ, their father, HAMID, and sister, AISHA.
ABDUL AZIZ has a beard and wears a Palestinian scarf with the rest of his Muslim attire.
Their father, HAMID, is wearing an old black suit and an orange v-neck jumper with shirt and tie underneath.
AISHA is in full black Jilbab (outer garment), black Hijab (head scarf) and black Nicaab (face veil).
HAMID has a Pakistani accent. ABDUL AZIZ and AISHA have broad Yorkshire accents.
Enter DAVID.

DAVID: Hello.

ABDUL AZIZ: Where is my sister?

DAVID: Jamillia?

ABDUL AZIZ: Yes!

DAVID: She's upstairs......... Praying.........

ABDUL AZIZ, AISHA and HAMID all look at one another in bewilderment.

...... Oh, it's OK...she's very safe...and I'm sure praying in privacy......... We were all quite taken with what a

decent person she is... You did a good job there, sir......
She's lovely!... I mean to say she's......a lovely......as in
good...... 'Muslim'...girl......we can all see that.........

*Suddenly, DAVID remembers the very large abstract contemporary
sculpture that is extremely erotic. Grabbing the damaged sheet he
quickly covers it. The two burnt holes are now eyeholes.*
*ABDUL AZIZ, AISHA and HAMID once again look at one another in
bewilderment.*

...... I'm sure anyone would love to have her as a
daughter-in-law......or...wife.

ABDUL AZIZ: Why do you say that?

DAVID: Well......you know......because of their –

HASSAN'S VOICE: Shut up!!!

*Enter SANJAY from one of the bedroom doors on the higher level.
He is now dressed in sexy, stylish and yet far more conservative
daywear.*
*After a moment of staring at JAMILLIA's family, he opens the bedroom
door again.*

SANJAY: Will you come out?!

HASSAN'S VOICE: I'm not coming out!

SANJAY: You have to.

HASSAN'S VOICE: No I don't!

SANJAY: They're your guests.

HASSAN'S VOICE: Guests!?... They're not my bloody guests!...
She called them...let her deal with them!

SANJAY: Well, it's your bloody mess.

HASSAN'S VOICE: I'm not coming out!!

SANJAY: Well, you'll have to at some point.

*SANJAY closes the bedroom door and starts to make his way down
stairs.*

HASSAN'S VOICE: Sanjay!

SANJAY goes back to the bedroom door and opens it.

SANJAY: Yes, master?

HASSAN'S VOICE: Have they taken their shoes off?

SANJAY: I think so.

HASSAN'S VOICE: Good!

SANJAY closes the bedroom door again and goes downstairs.

SANJAY: Hello!

ABDUL AZIZ: Astaghfirullah!!

SANJAY: Would you like a cup of tea while you wait?......

No reply.

...... Cup of tea?......

No reply.

...... No cup of tea......... They don't say much.

HAMID: This is a lovely house.

DAVID: Yeah…he's a lucky bastard, isn't he?!... I mean, yes, it's very nice.

ABDUL AZIZ: He?

SANJAY: My master. It's a fetish we have.

ABDUL AZIZ: Astaghfirullah!

DAVID: Mind you…his other properties aren't this nice.

SANJAY: Oh, no, no!... Those are for less deserving souls...... Those are for tenants...... This is his fortress…from which he rules his empire.

DAVID: Which you keep clean.

THE GREAT EXTENSION: ACT ONE

SANJAY: Which I keep in order, darling...... Without me this place would fall apart.

DAVID: Yeah...and I'm the one who stops his other properties from falling apart...they're a right mess, I tell yah.

HAMID: And you're having work done.

DAVID: Yes...extending, no less.

SANJAY: We like to be able to spread our feet.

DAVID: I always wanted a bachelor pad like this...but then it happened.

HAMID: What?

DAVID: Marriage.

HASSAN'S VOICE: Shut up!!

ABDUL AZIZ: Who is that man?!... And where is my sister?!

SANJAY: Will you get out here!... Now!!

Suddenly we hear music – it is mediocre jazz.
Enter HASSAN through the bedroom door on the upper floor wearing an elaborate dressing gown and cravat.
He lights a large Havana cigar and inhales but at once starts coughing because of the smoke. He quickly hides his inexperience with this symbol of refinement. HASSAN walks along the upper platform inspecting the books on the shelves. He picks one up and flicks through it.

Don't pretend you're reading it...

HASSAN gives SANJAY a dirty look then puts the book back in its place. He continues along the upper platform till he gets to the large antique telescope at which he stops and attempts to look through it.

...... It doesn't work!...

HASSAN gives SANJAY another dirty look.

... Get down here.

HASSAN comes down the staircase to the lower level.

HASSAN: David, my son…how is my extension?

DAVID: Hey?

HASSAN: My extension?… How is it?

DAVID: Fine… Everything is going to plan so far, Mr Hassan… All the boys are hard at work.

HASSAN: That's what I like to hear……… Well, shall we check, shall we?

HASSAN makes a poor attempt at exiting through the patio doors.

SANJAY: Get here and say hello!

HASSAN: Oh, I'm sorry!… Didn't see you there……… Welcome!… Welcome to my humble abode!……

HASSAN shakes HAMID's hand and then that of a reluctant ABDUL AZIZ. Finally, confused with what he should do with AISHA, he settles for a:

…… Hello.

ABDUL AZIZ: As-Salaamu Alaikum.

HASSAN: Absolutely.

Slight pause.

HAMID: We would like to see my daughter.

HASSAN: Ah…… She's upstairs……praying…… She won't be long……… That's where we keep the prayer mats… because…………well, that's just where we keep them.

HAMID: So, you pray?

HASSAN: Oh, when in need…when in need……… I've been praying all bloody morning.

HAMID: Subhanallah.

HASSAN: Exactly.

HAMID: What is all that?

HASSAN: It's......erm......art.

HAMID: Yes... I noticed those......very nice... They remind me of my own work.

DAVID: You're an artist?

HAMID: Well...a poet actually...or at least was... But once a poet, always a poet, I always say... But I studied calligraphy and painting too...as a child.

ABDUL AZIZ: I'm guessing you are a Sufi.

HASSAN: Well... I like to collect...some would say I'm an expert –

ABDUL AZIZ: A Sufi!

HASSAN: You what?

ABDUL AZIZ: You are a Sufi!

HASSAN: Am I?

SANJAY: Yes!

HASSAN: I suppose so, yeah.

ABDUL AZIZ: Astaghfirullah!

HASSAN: Yeah!

SANJAY: Will you help me, David?

DAVID: With what?

SANJAY: You'll see.

> *Pause.*
> *As HASSAN is left in an uncomfortable silence with JAMILLIA's family, we watch DAVID help SANJAY empty all the house of bottles of alcoholic drinks.*

HASSAN: Terrible weather we've been having.

ABDUL AZIZ: It's all from Allah.

HASSAN: Yeah?……

Slight pause.

…… They say it's global warming.

ABDUL AZIZ: From Allah!……

Slight pause.

…… If they followed the rules of Allah……they'd be no global warming.

HASSAN: Really?

ABDUL AZIZ: Yes!…… Look at swine flu…… If they never ate pigs…there'd be no swine flu.

Slight pause.

HASSAN: What about the Mad Cow's Disease, then?

Slight pause.

HAMID: Your parents…they are… Turkish?

HASSAN: Turkish…yes.

HAMID: We are Pakistani.

HASSAN: Lovely.

ABDUL AZIZ: Abba!… We are Muslim.

HAMID: Muslim, yes……but Pakistani.

HASSAN: Hey!… You say 'Baba'!… We say 'Baba'!

ABDUL AZIZ: 'Abba'!… I said 'Abba'!

HASSAN: Oh.

HAMID: But we say 'baba' too.

HASSAN: Lovely.

AISHA: Books!

HASSAN: Jesus!… You scared the shit out of me!

ABDUL AZIZ: Astaghfirullah!

HASSAN: You can say that again!

ABDUL AZIZ: Didn't you think she had a mouth?

HASSAN: Well, I don't know!… I can't see it, can I!

ABDUL AZIZ: It doesn't mean it's not there.

HASSAN: That's easy for you to say…you've seen it!

AISHA: I was commenting on your books.

HASSAN: What about them?!

AISHA: You have a good collection.

HASSAN: Have I?

AISHA: What's your taste?

HASSAN: Well………

Slight pause.

…… I'm quite partial to brandy, myself…… But I didn't think you lot would –

SANJAY: She's asking what you like to read.

HASSAN: You what?!

SANJAY: Read!… She's asking what you like to read.

HASSAN: Well……… Depends what frame of mind I'm in.

AISHA: Your taste in History?

HASSAN: Depends where I've been.

AISHA: Geography?

HASSAN: Depends where I'm at.

AISHA: Politics?

HASSAN: Depends who I've been talking to!... Look!... It's only bloody books!

AISHA: Only books!?... What a stupid thing to say.

HASSAN: I tell you what!... For someone with no mouth, she don't half talk a lot!

SANJAY: Master!

SANJAY turns off music.
Enter JAMILLIA from one of the bedroom doors.

HAMID: Jamillia!

HASSAN: Ah!... Here she is......... And here they are!... Your family!... Jamillia.........

Slight pause.

...... God, that's a pretty name!

DAVID: Very pretty.

HASSAN: I wish you'd stop doing that... What are you, a parrot?!

DAVID: What?... I'm just commenting on her name.

HASSAN: Well, don't!... She's not your –

SANJAY: Property to comment on.

HASSAN: No... She's not.

SANJAY: Because if she was...you might get possessive...like some.

HASSAN: I'm not getting possessive.

SANJAY: Yes you are!

HASSAN: Oh, shut up, you tart!

HAMID: Can we talk to my daughter, please?

HASSAN: Of course, mate...you go ahead.

Pause.

SANJAY: I think they want to be alone with her.

HASSAN: Sure!… I don't mind.

SANJAY: They want us to leave.

HASSAN: What!?

SANJAY: They want us to leave so they can be alone.

HASSAN: Bloody cheeky, innit?

SANJAY: Come on!

HASSAN: Alright!

DAVID: I can show you the tiles that were delivered this morning, if you like?

SANJAY: Ooh!… The 'Ostrich Plume'!?

DAVID: The off-white ones, yeah.

HASSAN: Sanjay?… Have you told them we've got a full inventory of the house?

SANJAY: Oh yeah!… I gave them a copy when they came in.

HASSAN: Just don't touch anything, OK.

Exit HASSAN, SANJAY and DAVID through the patio doors.

Pause.

HAMID: Jamillia.

JAMILLIA: Abba.

JAMILLIA comes down the stairs.

AISHA: Hey, girl!… I see you're getting down with the style on the street.

JAMILLIA: Well… I've got my big sister to look up to, innit.

AISHA: Innit!

HAMID: You look fantastic, Jamillia.

JAMILLIA: Do I?

HAMID: Different......but fantastic.

JAMILLIA: Oh, Abba!

JAMILLIA and her father, HAMID, embrace one another.

HAMID: As-Salaamu Alaikum, my daughter.

JAMILLIA: Alaikum Salaam, Abba.

HAMID: When you called and I heard your voice on the phone... I thought my heart was going to stop... But I didn't mind one bit...because I was already in heaven... Just the sound of your voice elevated me to paradise...my little angel.

JAMILLIA: Then you know how good it felt for me to finally hear your voice, Abba... I missed you so much.

HAMID: Then why didn't you call earlier?

JAMILLIA: A mixture of shame...and not being ready.

HAMID: And now?... Now you are ready?

JAMILLIA: I think so... I called, didn't I?

ABDUL AZIZ: Where the hell have you been?!

JAMILLIA: Oh, shut up!

HAMID: Now take it easy... OK?... Let's not fight... We can take this nice and easy... OK?... Now...... Where the hell have you been, Jamillia?!

ABDUL AZIZ: He's been worried sick about you!

JAMILLIA: I've been worried sick about me!

ABDUL AZIZ: Typical!... Selfish to the last drop!

JAMILLIA: Selfish?!

ABDUL AZIZ: Selfish!!… Selfish!… Selfish!… Selfish!

HAMID: If you have been anything, Jamillia… I can categorically say…that without any doubt…it is…selfish.

ABDUL AZIZ: Selfish!!… Selfish!… Selfish!… Selfish!

JAMILLIA: Will you shut up!

AISHA: Yes, I wish you would, Abdul Aziz…… I'm getting quite seasick with all this selfish.

ABDUL AZIZ: Oh! Are you?!… Well, maybe you're feeling sick because of all that Halva you ate on the way here!… She made me stop at every Indian sweet store between here and Brick Lane!… Not only did she have to sample every type but she had to buy a ton of the stuff as well!… And it all went down her gob by the time we got here!… I tell you what…it's a good job they can't see what you look like!

AISHA: Oh, you can be so cruel, Abdul Aziz.

JAMILLIA: Have you put on some weight?

AISHA: Just a couple of pounds.

ABDUL AZIZ: Couple of pounds?!… If she gets any bigger we'll need the Millennium Dome to cover her up!

HAMID: Well…they'll have to do something with it.

AISHA: They already have… It's the O2 Arena…the most popular music venue in the world.

HAMID: Really?… Everything is changing so quickly… I can't keep up with it all.

AISHA: Mind you… I wouldn't mind a bit of Take That up my jilbab.

ABDUL AZIZ: They wouldn't fit… We can hardly get you in there.

JAMILLIA: Oh, leave her alone!… You're nothing but a big bully!

ABDUL AZIZ: Oh really!?... Says she who has turned our lives upside-down... Selfish!... That's what you are... Selfish!... Selfish!... Selfish!

AISHA: Again with the selfish!

ABDUL AZIZ: Shut up!

JAMILLIA: You shut up!

Enter SANJAY from the patio doors. He walks over to the kitchen area and picks up an impressive piece of wood.

SANJAY: Sorry!... Need to see the Japanese Hinoki up against the Ostrich Plume.

Exit SANJAY from the patio doors.

ABDUL AZIZ: Astaghfirullah!

Pause.

HAMID: Where have you been, Jamillia?

JAMILLIA: Here in London.

ABDUL AZIZ: But where?!

JAMILLIA: None of your business!

ABDUL AZIZ: None of my business?!... I'm your brother and I'll slap you in a minute!

JAMILLIA: Yeah?!... Try it and I'll floor you!

ABDUL AZIZ: You see, Abba!... I told you and I told you!... Self-defence classes will get us nowhere!

HAMID: Why did you run away?

JAMILLIA: Why?

ABDUL AZIZ: Yes!... Why?!

JAMILLIA: Because I didn't want to go to Pakistan.

HAMID: That is our home.

JAMILLIA: No!… This is my home!

HAMID: Farrukh is a good boy……from a good family.

JAMILLIA: I know!… *Our* family!… I'm not going to let you take me halfway around the world to a place where I've never been to marry someone I've never seen…who happens to be my cousin!

AISHA: He's cute, you know.

JAMILLIA: I don't care!

AISHA: Sure?

JAMILLIA: Yes!

AISHA: Then you don't mind if I have him?

JAMILLIA: Go for it, sis.

AISHA: I told you she wouldn't mind!

HAMID & ABDUL AZIZ: Shut up!

HAMID: You have always been a rebel.

JAMILLIA: Abba… I don't want to marry someone just because of cultural pressures… I would have thought you of all people would understand that.

Slight pause.

HAMID: Why didn't you talk to us?… We wouldn't have forced you to do anything you didn't want to do.

JAMILLIA: Rukhsana tried talking to her parents……and look what happened to her.

ABDUL AZIZ: I don't want to talk about that… Never talk about that!

AISHA: I miss Rukhsana.

ABDUL AZIZ: Don't talk about her!

HAMID: She was a good girl.

JAMILLIA: And look what happened to her…all because of her parents.

HAMID: Her parents wanted the best for her.

JAMILLIA: Her parents wanted her to go to Pakistan and marry her cousin.

AISHA: They didn't give her much choice.

JAMILLIA: Yeah…… And look what happened.

ABDUL AZIZ: Stop it!… I don't want to hear about her… Don't you understand?!

HAMID: Family is family.

JAMILLIA: Exactly.… Family is family.… Not marrying material.… Things have changed since your time, abba… We are now in this country and we should have the choice of following our true feelings.

AISHA: Poor Rukhsana.

JAMILLIA: Who would have thought?

ABDUL AZIZ: Stop it!… She's gone and that's it!

HAMID: Who would have thought she'd go to such drastic levels?

JAMILLIA: It happens…much more than you think.

HAMID: I know!… I know!……

Slight pause.

…… But to run off and marry an Englishman!

AISHA: A kafir!

ABDUL AZIZ: And gave him six sons!

ABDUL AZIZ, HAMID, AISHA & JAMILLIA: Astaghfirullah!!

ABDUL AZIZ: God, I miss her!

JAMILLIA: I know… You were close.

AISHA: But she's gone now.

HAMID: And that is that.

Suddenly, we hear the electronic chime of 'Jerusalem' by William Blake.

ABDUL AZIZ: What the hell is that?

JAMILLIA: There's somebody at the door.

Slight pause.

HAMID: Well, who's going to answer it?

AISHA: Do you want me to get it?

HAMID & ABDUL AZIZ: No!

JAMILLIA: I'll get it.

JAMILLIA exits to answer the front door as her family begin to snoop around.

MR BROWN'S VOICE: Where's Marigold? You'll have to learn English if you're going to answer the door.

Enter MR BROWN holding the land deeds.

MR BROWN: Jesus Christ!

HAMID: Sorry… You're in the wrong house…… You want Jesus Christ…try the next house down.

MR BROWN: I live in the next house down!

HAMID: Well, like I said…you're in the wrong house.

HAMID and his children all laugh at his wit.

MR BROWN: Where's Mr Hassan?!… He's not in there, is he?!

ABDUL AZIZ: That's my sister!

MR BROWN: Is it?

ABDUL AZIZ: Yes!

MR BROWN: Well, what have you done with Mr Hassan?!

HAMID: We haven't done anything with him.

MR BROWN: Where is he then?!

ABDUL AZIZ: He's out there.

HAMID: Checking his Japanese Hinoki up against the Ostrich Plume.

MR BROWN: Oh yeah!?… What's that then, hey?!… Islamic?!

HAMID: No!… Eclectic.

MR BROWN: Right!… You… Abdul… Go and get him.

ABDUL AZIZ: You what?

MR BROWN: Go and get Mr Hassan.

ABDUL AZIZ: Do I know you?

MR BROWN: No you bloody don't!

ABDUL AZIZ: Well, how do you know my name?

MR BROWN: You what?

ABDUL AZIZ: You just called me 'Abdul'.

MR BROWN: Oh, my God……… It's a figure of speech!

AISHA: Figure of speech?!

MR BROWN: Jesus!!… It just scared the shit out of me!!

ABDUL AZIZ: 'It'?!… Astaghfirullah!!

MR BROWN: You can say that again!

ABDUL AZIZ: What's the matter with you people?!… Why are you so surprised she's got a mouth?!

MR BROWN: Well, we can't see it, can we!

ABDUL AZIZ: That doesn't mean it's not there!

MR BROWN: That's easy for you to say!... You've seen it!......

Slight pause.

...... It's alright, love... We'll save you from the shackles of your religion.

AISHA: You what?!

MR BROWN: It's alright...... I know you can't talk......not while they're around.

AISHA: You stupid jerk!

MR BROWN: Who said that?

ABDUL AZIZ: Astaghfirullah!... She did!... My sister!

MR BROWN: What did she call me?

HAMID: A stupid jerk.

MR BROWN: Can she say that?

ABDUL AZIZ: She just did!

MR BROWN: Bloody cheek!... I know you're putting on a façade for their sake... But you don't have to be so harsh, love.

AISHA: I have no shackles to my religion!

MR BROWN: I know... I know... You won't have to keep this up for much longer, girl...... We'll have you out of there in no time.

AISHA: Do you ever read, you stupid jerk?!

MR BROWN: Listen!... I told you...less of the 'jerk'!... Alright?

AISHA: Do you ever read?!

MR BROWN: Read?!

AISHA: Yes!

MR BROWN: Well…… Sometimes…… Depends what frame of mind I'm in………

AISHA proceeds to go up the stairs to the upper floor.

…… Can she go up there?

ABDUL AZIZ: Yes!… She's got legs too!

AISHA: My religion hasn't given me shackles… It's given me rights… Rights!… Muslim women have enjoyed rights that were given to them one-thousand-four-hundred years ago…rights that Western women do not enjoy even today…or if they do…the so called 'women's liberation movement' only obtained them at the beginning of the twentieth century!

ABDUL AZIZ: You hear that!… Subhanallah!

Enter HASSAN, SANJAY and DAVID from the patio doors.

HASSAN: Oi! What's he doing in here? And what's she doing up there? Sanjay!

AISHA: Rights such as 'the vote'… being able to voice their opinions and participate in politics!

ABDUL AZIZ: That's right, Aisha…… That's right!

While ranting, AISHA searches for the right books along the library and then takes them off the shelves making a pile in her arms.

HASSAN: Oi!… Leave my bloody books alone!… Sanjay!… She's messing them all up!

MR BROWN: Leave her!… She's only putting on an act for them.

AISHA: Human rights!… Unlike some religions… Islam tells us that women are not evil by nature…since both men and women came from the same essence…they are equal in their humanity!

ABDUL AZIZ: You tell them sister!… You tell them!

AISHA: The right to be educated… In fact, this is pretty much an obligation since the prophet Muhammad –

ABDUL AZIZ & AISHA: Sallallaahu alaihi wasallam! –

AISHA: Said 'Heaven lies at the feet of mothers'…of course telling us that the success of a society can be traced to the mothers that raised it!

ABDUL AZIZ: My sister is on a roll!

HASSAN: You must be bloody joking!… She hasn't seen my mother!… My books, Sanjay!… My books!

AISHA descends back down the stairs with the pile of books.

AISHA: But the right that comes to mind most……is the basic freedom of 'expression'!… And you…'Mr next door neighbour'…are a stupid jerk!……

AISHA dumps the books into MR BROWN's arms.

…… Read!… Just read!

Slight pause.

MR BROWN: She is good though, ain't she……… It's almost like she means it.

HASSAN: Give me those!……

HASSAN grabs the books out of MR BROWN's hands and puts them down on a nearby surface.

…… Now!… You are all my guests… And welcome to you all… But if you don't stick to my rules…leave my stuff alone…and make a bloody mess…then you know what you can all do, don't yah?!… You can all –

SANJAY: Fun! Have lots and lots of fun! Master!… Remember why they are here.

Slight pause.

HASSAN: Jamillia!

SANJAY: Well done.........

JAMILLIA is flicking through the books which have been brought down from the library. HASSAN watches her.

...... Right...would anyone like that cup of tea now?

MR BROWN: Oh, a cup of tea!... That would be lovely!

SANJAY: I wasn't asking you... I'm asking the guests.

MR BROWN: Well what the bloody hell am I?

AISHA: A stupid jerk!

MR BROWN: Who said that?

ABDUL AZIZ: Astaghfirullah!

SANJAY: Cup of tea!?

DAVID: Is it me or do they keep ignoring you?

SANJAY: Oh, they always ignore my kind...unless they want something.

DAVID: Anyone for a cup of tea?!

HAMID, ABDUL AZIZ & AISHA: Yes please!

SANJAY proceeds to make tea for everyone.
HASSAN is still observing JAMILLIA.

HASSAN: Well...... I've met your folks.

JAMILLIA: Yes...you have.

Slight pause.

HASSAN: They're...er............lovely.

JAMILLIA: You really think so?

HASSAN: Yeah!... Lovely.........

Slight pause.

...... You comfortable?

JAMILLIA: What do you mean?

HASSAN: Here?… Are you comfortable…here?… I want you to feel at home.

JAMILLIA: At home?

HASSAN: Well…you know………till we sort things out.

Slight pause.

JAMILLIA: I'm very comfortable.

Slight pause.

HASSAN: What is it about you?… Every time I talk to you… I get the munchies.

JAMILLIA: The munchies?

HASSAN: Oh, sorry……… Every time I talk to you……… I feel like…munching on something sweet.

ABDUL AZIZ: Oi!… I heard that!

HASSAN: You heard what!?

ABDUL AZIZ: That's my sister!

HASSAN: What?!

ABDUL AZIZ: You said…every time you talk to her you feel like munching on something sweet…… Astaghfirullah!

DAVID: You didn't say that, did you?

HASSAN: No!… Well, yes!… But not in the way he means it!

MR BROWN: You bloody pervert!

HASSAN: I'm not a bloody pervert!

SANJAY: Yes you are… And I wouldn't have you any other way.

HASSAN: Oh shut up Sanjay! For once and for all!… What I meant was…every time I talk to her… I feel like…eating something sweet –

81

ABDUL AZIZ: Astaghfirullah! –

HASSAN: As in a dessert!

ABDUL AZIZ: You just stay away from my sister!... I don't
know what she's doing here...but you just stay away!...
You hear me?!

Slight pause.

HAMID: What is she doing here?... No one has told us yet.

DAVID: Mate, now's your chance?

HASSAN: Sanjay!... What about that cup of tea, hey! And
make sure you give them all coasters.

HAMID: Well, what is she doing here?

*Suddenly, we hear the electronic chime of 'Jerusalem' by William
Blake.*

HASSAN: Ah!... There's somebody at the door... Saved by the
bell.

SANJAY: That'll be your parents.

HASSAN: Fuck!!... What are they doing here?!!... She didn't
call them as well, did she?

SANJAY: Oh, no...... I called them... I mean, a party wouldn't
be a party without the Peckham Hassans, now would it......
'Munch on something sweet'... You dotty amnesiac!... I'm
getting sick of dealing with the relics of your insobriety...
It was a fetish that is no more!... This is one booty that
has made the trannie pop!... It's time you woke up to
remember what you desire.

*SANJAY exits to answer the front door leaving HASSAN wincing
with frustration.*

JAMILLIA: Are you alright?

HASSAN: I'm sorry.

JAMILLIA: For what?

HASSAN: I'm so bloody sorry.

JAMILLIA: I don't understand.

HASSAN: You'll see.

Act Two

SANJAY'S VOICE: Ahh!

Enter SANJAY, rubbing his bottom.
Enter HASSAN's parents, MR & MRS HASSAN.
MR HASSAN is dressed in a Savile Row tailored suit and carries
Turkish worry beads. He is a tall handsome man with a neatly
trimmed thin moustache and has an accent.
MRS HASSAN is an elegant lady who is dressed very stylishly but yet
conservatively. Although stylish and conservative, MRS HASSAN is
reserved to the point of almost hiding something – she is pissed.

HASSAN: Hello, Baba –

MR HASSAN: Shut up!… Sanjay, put the radio on… Quick!

SANJAY: Yes, master-baba.

SANJAY picks up a remote-control and turns on the radio.

NEWS BULLETIN: And in Ankara, President Barack Obama laid a wreath at the mausoleum of Mustafa Kemal Ataturk –

MR HASSAN: Ataturk! –

NEWS BULLETIN: The leader of the Turkish war of independence and the founder of the Turkish republic. –

MR HASSAN: You're damn right, baby! –

NEWS BULLETIN: Praising modern Turkey's founder Mustafa Kemal Ataturk as a 'man with vision, tenacity and courage who put Turkey on the path of democracy,' –

MR HASSAN: You hear that?!… You hear that?! –

NEWS BULLETIN: Obama quoted one of the most popular sayings of Ataturk in the memorial book –

MR HASSAN & NEWS BULLETIN: 'Peace at home, peace in the world' –

'Peace at home, peace in the world' –

MR HASSAN: He's a good man, that Obama, ha!

NEWS BULLETIN: Under heavy security measures, Obama
  proceeded from Ataturk's mausoleum to the presidential
  palace where he was warmly greeted by President
  Abdullah Gul. –

MR HASSAN: Hade, be Gul! –

NEWS BULLETIN: He was honoured with a 21-gun salute but
  was stunned by the noise from the first shot.

MR HASSAN: Hah!!… Fucking American yank!… He's
  frightened of Turkish guns!

NEWS BULLETIN: Although President Obama was visiting the
  hub of Turkish secularism, his counterpart, President Gul
  has been at the centre of crisis in recent years of Turkish
  politics.

MR HASSAN: What?!

NEWS BULLETIN: The choice of his wife to wear the headscarf
  had plunged the country into the most serious political
  and economic crisis for years, even prompting fears of a
  military coup.

MR HASSAN: Ah!… They always have to tell the world this
  shit!

NEWS BULLETIN: Turkey's powerful military high command
  had come out publicly against Mr Gul's candidature,
  and hundreds of thousands of protesters had taken to the
  streets voicing their fear that Mr Gul's AK party's agenda
  is to move Turkey towards a more conservative, Islamic,
  society –

MR HASSAN: Never!!

NEWS BULLETIN: And that the headscarf is one of the most
  visible and symbolic elements of its agenda. Turkish
  women who cover their hair because of their Islamic

beliefs say the restrictions on the headscarf have blocked generations of religiously conservative women from higher education.

MR HASSAN: Ah, fuck off!

NEWS BULLETIN: Turkey's military, however, sees itself as the guardian of Ataturk's secular laws and principles.

MR HASSAN: Damn right, baby!… Ataturk!!

NEWS BULLETIN: The hot debate goes on.

MR HASSAN grabs the remote-control and turns the radio off.

MR HASSAN: Hello!… Hello! Hello! Hello!……

MR HASSAN walks over and grabs AISHA by the hand.

There is a gasp of breath from everyone else.

…… You see that, Hassan!…no pump…no crush……and no lingering…… Never kiss a woman's hand if you are English…… But…of course…us being continental…we can!……

MR HASSAN kisses AISHA's hand. There is another gasp of breath from the others.

…… But!… Never kiss a single girl's hand… This treatment is reserved for married women only……… Are you married?

HAMID: No, she's not.

MR HASSAN: Ah…… Well anyway…you shouldn't offer your hand unless a woman extends hers first.

HASSAN: But, baba!… She didn't offer her hand.

MR HASSAN: Shush! I'm trying to teach you about etiquette here, be Hassan.

HASSAN: Yes, baba.

ABDUL AZIZ: Astaghfirullah! Jamillia get your stuff we're going.

MR HASSAN: Ah!!... You are Muslims!... I would never have been able to tell.

HAMID: Are you Muslims?

MR HASSAN: Of course... El-humdulillah.

HAMID: I really wouldn't have been able to tell.

MR HASSAN: Right!... I'm Mr Hassan...and this delightful lady, is Mrs Hassan,... We are Hassan's parents.

HASSAN: Yep!

MR HASSAN: So!... What is the problem?...... Where are you from?... Lewisham?... Eltham?... Catford?...... And more importantly...what do you want?...

HASSAN: But, Baba!

MR HASSAN: Shut up and learn, be Hassan... I have many years experience of dealing with tenants.

HASSAN: Baba!

MR HASSAN: Shut up!!...... Tell me!... What do you want!?

HAMID: We don't won't anything.

MR HASSAN: Don't want anything?!

ABDUL AZIZ: We are not tenants!

MR HASSAN: Not tenants?

HAMID: No!

ABDUL AZIZ: Why did you say we look like tenants?

MR HASSAN: What?

ABDUL AZIZ: You said we look like tenants.

MR HASSAN: Well!...... You know.

HAMID: 'You know' what?

MR HASSAN: Well......the way one looks is very important.

HAMID: The way one looks?

MR HASSAN: Like someone's manners...someone's clothes are a good sign to who they are.

HAMID: Who they are?

MR HASSAN: What else have other people to go on when trying to work out your character...but for the way you look?

ABDUL AZIZ: It's true.

DAVID: Where do you get all this stuff about character and the way you look?

MR HASSAN: Ah!... That is a good question, David...... From my *Gentleman's book of Etiquette*.

HASSAN: Published 1924.

MR HASSAN: I brought up all my children on it.

HASSAN: Yep!

ABDUL AZIZ: Astaghfirullah!... I only agreed with you because it says that too in the Koran and the Sunnah...the ways of our prophet –

AISHA & ABDUL AZIZ: Sallallaahu alaihi wasallam

MR HASSAN: Ah...the Koran...our beloved book......yes that is a good book too.

ABDUL AZIZ: A good book?!... That is the word of God!

MR HASSAN: Of course.

HAMID: I am no tenant!... I am proud to say I own my own house.

MR HASSAN: I am proud to say we own twenty-two of our own houses.

MR BROWN: Yeah…and the poor suffering bastards living in them.

MR HASSAN: And who is this, Hassan?… Is he a tenant?

MR BROWN: No I'm bloody not!… I live next door…in my own property.

MR HASSAN: Well, what are you doing here then?… You are in the wrong house.

HAMID: I already told him that. Jamillia!

HASSAN: What are you doing here, Mr Brown?

MR BROWN: I came to tell you that someone has parked on the grass on the land between our houses…… I'm sorry… but that's not yours to park on.

MR HASSAN: That's our land!

MR BROWN: No it's not!… No decision has been made yet.

MR HASSAN: We're going to extend on that land.

MR BROWN: Not before any decision is made you're not… I have the original deeds to the land here…and I think you'll find that it is my land.

MR HASSAN: Hah!… The original deeds?… Yes, I've seen those… I'm sorry to inform you but those are forgeries –

MR BROWN: Forgeries?

MR HASSAN: That's right… Something about someone regretting selling the land and then substituting the genuine deeds with those forgeries to claim the land back –

MR BROWN: That's rubbish!

MR HASSAN: That's right…complete rubbish… Time has a way of clouding the truth until it's nothing but speculation… Depends on who's telling the story… And right now the story goes that those deeds are forgeries… and the land…the land is ours.

MR BROWN: Right!… Whosever car that is I'd like them to move it!… Now!… I'm guessing it's Bob the builder's.

MR HASSAN: 'Bob the builder'?

DAVID: It's not mine… I come here in my van…… And my name is 'David'!

HAMID: I think you're talking about my car. The Mercedes?

MR BROWN: Yes!

HAMID: Yes. That's my car.

MR HASSAN: You?… You drive a Mercedes?

HAMID: Yes, actually… I do……… My son bought it for me… He is in computers.

MR HASSAN: You?

ABDUL AZIZ: Yes!… And you?!… What do you do?!

Slight pause.

HASSAN: He's in property!

MR HASSAN: Yes…that's right!… I'm in property…… This is one of ours.

MR BROWN: Yeah, you wanna to see the others…and the poor bastards that live in 'em.

MR HASSAN: I don't like you!

MR BROWN: I don't like you!… I don't like any of you.

MR HASSAN: What is your name, sir?!

MR BROWN: Brown!… Mr Brown!

HAMID: That is the trouble with this country…too many browns.

MRS HASSAN stumbles.

SANJAY: Oh the poor dear, shall I get you a blanket? She trained at one of the best conservatoires in the world you know.

MR HASSAN: In Turkey!

SANJAY: She used to be an opera singer...didn't you, darling?

HAMID: How lovely......another artist.

MR HASSAN: Yes...well...that was a long time ago, wasn't it, 'darling'... Everything changes when you get married.

HAMID: Yes... I'm afraid to say...that is true.

MR HASSAN: It's always the case.

SANJAY: Ahh!

SANJAY has just walked past MR HASSAN as he serves up some more tea. He walks off rubbing his bottom.

AISHA: Why?

MR HASSAN: Who said that?

AISHA: Me?

MR HASSAN: What did you say?

AISHA: Why does everything have to change when you get married?

MR HASSAN: Because that's how it is?

AISHA: That's how what is?

MR HASSAN: It.

AISHA: It?

MR HASSAN: Yes!... 'It'!... 'It'!

AISHA: 'It' is a God-given right for a woman to have an education and the independence to work!

MR HASSAN: Independence to work!?... Don't be so stupid.

AISHA: Stupid!!

AISHA runs up the stairs to the library.

HASSAN: Oh, my God!... Here she goes again!... Sanjay!

HAMID: Don't worry... It's good for her... She'll lose some
weight.

ABDUL AZIZ: That's true.

MR BROWN: Poor girl... She'll do anything to convince us that
she believes in all that crap

HASSAN: Sanjay!... My books!

AISHA pulls another book out and brings it back down the stairs.

SANJAY: Well, at least someone is making use of them.

HASSAN: Making use of them? She's making a bloody mess,
that's what she's doing!

AISHA: Read, Mr Hassan!... Read!... It is a God-given right
for a woman to have an education and the independence
to work!

HASSAN: Give me that!

MR HASSAN: Ah!... But who wrote that book?... Maybe that
too is a forgery... Have you thought of that?

MR HASSAN: Listen, young lady! –

MR BROWN: Young lady?... How can you tell!? Could be
bloody anyone in there!... Her and her mates could be
taking shifts in there while your daughter is out on the
tiles... Have you thought of that?

HAMID & ABDUL AZIZ: Astaghfirullah!!

Slight pause.

HAMID: Aisha?

AISHA: Don't worry, Abba......it's me!

HAMID: Good girl.

MR HASSAN: Listen, young lady......you will realise that when you get married –

AISHA: You will realise...and men like you...that I will practise my God-given right to work...and I won't be enslaved to his name... 'Mr and Mrs Hassan'!

MR HASSAN: What do you mean by that?

AISHA: I will keep my own name.

MR HASSAN: What!?... That's disgusting!... Don't be so stupid!... If that was the case my wife wouldn't have the privilege of being a 'Hassan', would she!?

HASSAN: She already was a 'Hassan'...remember?

MR HASSAN: Oh, yes.

AISHA: I will keep my name...and...the right to work... therefore I will keep my business!

MR BROWN: Business?

HAMID: That's right... My daughter has her own business.

MR BROWN: In what!?

AISHA: Cosmetics.

MR BROWN: Cos-bloody-metics!

AISHA: That's right.

HAMID: She's wearing half-a-ton of the stuff right now.

ABDUL AZIZ: Abba!

MR BROWN: Why!?... I mean, what's the bloody point?!

AISHA: Listen!... We don't always wear this, you know.

MR HASSAN: But who's going to see you?

AISHA: My family!… Oh! And just maybe the other half of the human race…you know…women!

MR HASSAN: Don't see the point, really.

MR BROWN: Not really, no.

AISHA: You are so stupid!

MR HASSAN: Who!?

AISHA: Men!!

MR HASSAN: For someone with no mouth, she don't half talk a lot.

HAMID: I have to live with her…… If only she would lose some weight…someone might have her –

AISHA & JAMILLIA: Abba!

MR BROWN: Listen!… Is someone going to move that car!?

ABDUL AZIZ: I'll move it, Browny…… Abba, the keys.

HAMID throws the car keys to ABDUL AZIZ.

MR HASSAN: Don't you bloody dare! That is our land and I say you can leave the Mercedes there.

MR BROWN: Abdul!… Move the car!

HASSAN: Abdul?… Do you two know each other?

MR BROWN: Oh, my God!… It's a figure of speech!… Have you lot never heard it?!… 'Hello, Abdul'!… 'Watch it, Abdul'!… 'Move the bloody car off my land, Abdul'!!

MR HASSAN: It's not your land!… It's our land!… And the Mercedes stays!

MR BROWN: Right!… I'll bloody move it myself, then!

MR BROWN grabs the keys out of ABDUL AZIZ's hand and rushes towards the patio doors.

ABDUL AZIZ: Oi!… Give me those back!

MR HASSAN: The Mercedes stays, I said!… It bloody stays!

HAMID: My Mercedes!… My Mercedes!

MR BROWN runs out of the patio doors quickly followed by MR HASSAN, ABDUL AZIZ and HAMID.

DAVID: Bloody hell!

DAVID and SANJAY have a quick glance at one another and then, not wanting to miss the action, they too run out of the patio doors.
Pause.
HASSAN and JAMILLIA stare at each other as AISHA looks on.

HASSAN: Is she watching us?… I can't tell……

JAMILLIA giggles.

… Don't you want to go out there?… You can see my extension.

AISHA: No thank you.

Slight pause.

HASSAN: You sure?

Slight pause.

AISHA: Stupid men!

Realising she's not wanted, AISHA too exits, staggering through the patio doors.
Pause.

HASSAN: Well…………… You've met my folks now.

JAMILLIA: Yep……… One of them is still here.

MRS HASSAN is sleeping on the chair.

HASSAN: I did already apologise… I will again if you like?

JAMILLIA: No need……… Nobody's perfect.

HASSAN: No……they're bloody not………

Pause.

...... It's really weird.........you're my wife.

JAMILLIA: Yes...... I am.

HASSAN: Although...they don't know it yet.

JAMILLIA: Not yet...no.

Slight pause.

HASSAN: Do you want to tell them?

JAMILLIA: I think...... I'll leave that to you.

HASSAN: Cheers.........

Pause.

...... My wife, hey?

JAMILLIA: Yeah.

HASSAN: Well.........we'll have it all sorted soon......and you can be on your way.

JAMILLIA: Yeah.............. You know... I never thought I'd be divorced.

HASSAN: Well...that's weird......... 'cause I never thought I'd be married.

JAMILLIA: But you are.

HASSAN: Yes.

Slight pause.

JAMILLIA: Don't you remember anything?

HASSAN: No... I don't...... I don't think I really want to.

JAMILLIA: No?

HASSAN: No.................. All I know is......every time I talk to you......all I want to do is munch on something sweet...

HASSAN opens the fridge and pulls out a big Black Forest Gateau cake. Grabbing a spoon he proceeds to munch away at it. A smile

comes up on JAMILLIA's face as she sneakily pours the remainder of
a bottle of alcohol into the teapot.
Behind, through the glass back wall, we suddenly see a Mercedes
erected up in the air.
Enter MR HASSAN, MR BROWN, ABDUL AZIZ, HAMID, AISHA,
DAVID and SANJAY.

ABDUL AZIZ: You stupid bloody Sufi!

MR HASSAN: I told you the Mercedes stays!

HAMID: My Mercedes!… What have you done to my
    Mercedes?!

MR HASSAN: I told you!… It's our land and the Mercedes
    stays!

MR BROWN: You fucking idiot!

HAMID: He's smashed my Mercedes!

HASSAN: Into what?!

ABDUL AZIZ: Into that fucking pit…… Astaghfirullah!

HASSAN: What fucking pit?!

ABDUL AZIZ: Why would you have such a thing?!… Is it a
    dugout?… Are you planning war?!… Is it Jihad?!… What's
    it there for?!

MR BROWN: Oh, it's a declaration of war, alright, mate!…
    they're extending.

HASSAN: Will someone tell me what the fuck is going on?!…
    David!!

    Slight pause.

DAVID: They've ploughed the Mercedes into the foundations.

MR BROWN: Fuck your foundations… It's still poking its arse
    out over the line into my land.

HASSAN: I'm going to fucking murder you!

HAMID: I'm going to call the police!

MR HASSAN: The police?!

HASSAN: No one is calling the police!

MR HASSAN: No... No... We don't need the police!

MR BROWN: Well...you're either going to push the whole thing into your fucking foundations...or have it removed... because it's still crossing over to my land.

HASSAN: Mr Brown!... Shut the fuck up!!

HAMID: No one is touching that car until what happened has been officially documented by the police.

MR HASSAN: That English racist hooligan tried to steal this poor Pakistani man's car.

MR BROWN: You bloody what?!

MR HASSAN: Everyone here is a witness... You grabbed the keys from this poor Muslim boy and tried to drive their car away.

MR BROWN: That's absolute bollocks!

MR HASSAN: Everyone here saw it.

ABDUL AZIZ: Yeah... And then you grabbed the steering wheel.

MR HASSAN: I tried to save your car.

HAMID: You veered it straight into the pit.

HASSAN: Foundation!... My foundation!... To my extension!

SANJAY: Oh!!... Been eating cake have we?!... Had the munchies have we?!... Somebody's been chatting!!

HASSAN: Oh, shut up you fucking tart!!

ABDUL AZIZ: You stupid Sufi!

MR HASSAN: Yes! I'm a Sufi!!… I'm a Turk!!… And you, 'Abdul', are a stupid Wahhabi!

ABDUL AZIZ: What did you say!?

DAVID: Tea's ready!… Why don't I pour us all a cup and then we can all calm down and deal with the matter in hand.

MR HASSAN: You think I'm stupid!?… You think I don't know what you are?… I knew as soon as I saw you what you was!… You're a Wahhabi!

ABDUL AZIZ: 'Wahhabi'!…… 'Wahhabi'!… 'Wahhabi'!… 'Wahhabi'!… That's all you people say… I'm a Salafi!… Someone who adheres to the way of the Salaf…the Prophet –

AISHA & ABDUL AZIZ: Sallallaahu alaihi Wasallam!

MR HASSAN: Yes, yes, yes!… You're a Wahhabi!… You follow the teachings of Ibn Abd al-Wahhab who formed an alliance with the British to overthrow the Ottoman Khilafah… And now you're forming an alliance with them to take the Mercedes off my land!

MR BROWN: It's not your land!

MR HASSAN: Yes it is!

HASSAN: It's my fucking extension!

HAMID: It's my Mercedes!

MR HASSAN, MR BROWN & HASSAN: Shut up!!

ABDUL AZIZ: Bloody Ottomans!… Sufis!

MR HASSAN: You ignorant pig!… Don't you dare say a thing about the Ottomans!… Everyone knows what the Ottomans did… It was us that spread Islam!… You ignorant pig!

ABDUL AZIZ: 'Spread Islam'!… It was Allah who spread Islam… The Ottomans spread nothing but their ostentatious spirituality…pretentious and flamboyant Sufi rubbish!

MR HASSAN: You pig!… You ignorant pig!… I bet you've never read a history book in your life!

ABDUL AZIZ: If you had you'd know your history!

MR HASSAN: Right!

ABDUL AZIZ: Right!

Both MR HASSAN and ABDUL AZIZ look up at the library. There is a moment of silence. Then, the race is on. They both run up the stairs trying to beet each other to the books.

HASSAN: What are they doing?!… Sanjay!!… Get them down from there!!

SANJAY: No!… *You* get them down!

HASSAN: Sanjay!!

MR HASSAN and ABDUL AZIZ are both pulling out books from the library as they rant and rave at each other.

ABDUL AZIZ: You'll see!… When we get our Khilafah you'll see what we'll do with you stinking Sufis…and the Shias!… You wait for the Islamic state!

MR HASSAN: The Khilafah!?… It was the Wahhabis who stabbed the Khilafah in the back in the first place…the Ottoman khilafah!… It was the Wahhabis who helped get rid of the Islamic state in the first place!

ABDUL AZIZ: You bloody Sufi!… I'm a Salafi!

MR HASSAN: Wahhabi!

ABDUL AZIZ: Salafi!

MR HASSAN: Wahhabi!!

MR BROWN: Is this what they mean by the Muslim brotherhood?

MR HASSAN & ABDUL AZIZ: El-humdulillah!!… Yes!!!

MR HASSAN and ABDUL AZIZ start throwing the books at each other bringing the argument to an all-time infantile peak.

HASSAN: Sanjay!!!

SANJAY: What!?

HASSAN: There's a ring stain on my table!!!!

SANJAY: Tough!

DAVID takes centre stage and takes his hard-hat off. On a string from around his neck, DAVID pulls out a whistle and blows on it hard. All falls silent. Slight pause.

DAVID: Is no one curious to why we are all here?

Pause. Everyone is staring at DAVID.

AISHA: What's that on your head?

DAVID: What?

DAVID is frozen to the spot, paranoid with what might be on his head.
DAVID slowly turns round to reveal he is wearing a Kippa, the Jewish men's headwear worn in respect for their faith.

MR BROWN: Jesus Christ!!… That's all we need!… Did you know this?!

DAVID: What is it?

HASSAN: What?!

MR BROWN: That Bob the builder is Jewish!

HASSAN: Well……it's the entertainment industry, innit!!… It's full of 'em!!

MR BROWN: Not 'Bob the Builder'!…'Bob'…the builder!

ABDUL AZIZ: Astaghfirullah!… You allow a Jew in your house?!

HASSAN: Oi!...leave him alone!

ABDUL AZIZ: Right!... Abba!... Let's go!

HAMID: What about my Mercedes?!

ABDUL AZIZ: Leave it!... I'll buy you another one.

MR BROWN: Oh, no you don't!... You're not leaving before you move that car off my land!

MR HASSAN: It's in my land!

HASSAN: It's in my foundations!... To my extension!

HAMID: I'm not going anywhere without my Mercedes!

ABDUL AZIZ: I won't spend a second under the same roof as a Jew!

MR HASSAN: That sounds good to me!... You know where the door is.

ABDUL AZIZ: Abba!!

HAMID: I'm not leaving without my Mercedes!

ABDUL AZIZ: But there's a Jew amongst us!

HAMID: Oh you silly boy!... There's always been Jews amongst us!

ABDUL AZIZ: Astaghfirullah!

DAVID: Listening to you all...there really isn't that much between us.

MR BROWN: Oh, I'll go along with that!... You all stink of the same conniving shit!

HASSAN: You what?

MR BROWN: Well... It's because of all you bloody Muslims and Jews that our civilization is dying... You Jews with your ulterior motives and you bloody Muslims with your

Dark Age Sharia laws… Islamitizing our lands, crushing our spirit and sending us straight back to the Dark Ages!

SANJAY: You are such a bigoted racist bastard!

MR BROWN: Oh, shut up, you poof!!

SANJAY: What did you call me?!

MR BROWN: A poof!… You're a bloody poof!… And I don't mean, 'Gay'… 'Gay' is our word that you lot hijacked… And it means, 'happy'… You are far from happy!… You are a poof!

SANJAY: I am not a poof!…

Slight pause as the others stare at SANJAY.

…… I'm not gay!…… I…am a transgender.

MR BROWN: Oh, fuck off!!

SANJAY: I…with my beautiful effeminate body…pursue gender reassignment… In a very straight world, I fulfil a very heterosexual fantasy… Just because we do it a lot better than you…it doesn't make us, 'gay'… Being 'Gay' is –

HAMID: A man's love and appreciation of another man.

SANJAY: 'Man' on 'man'…… Now tell me…do I look like a man to you?

MR BROWN: So what does that make you?

HASSAN: Who?

MR BROWN: You!?

HASSAN: Me?!

MR BROWN: Yes, you!

Slight pause.

HASSAN: I'm a man...... As in, just a man...... You know...an ordinary man.

MR BROWN: Ordinary?

HASSAN: Of course, I'm bloody ordinary!

MR BROWN: Really?

Slight pause as HASSAN thinks.

HASSAN: That's disgusting!... Of course, I'm a man!... Baba!

MR HASSAN: Hey!... My son is a man!... A lazy good for nothing piece of shit!...

HASSAN: Yeah... No!

MR HASSAN: ... But...a man!... Listen...if I can't find a nice luxury marble toilet to poo in and I go and shit in some bush...does that make me a bush?... No... I am still a man...no matter where I shit... I am still a man.

HAMID: You...are a fool, my friend...... Allow me to apologise, Sanjay.

ABDUL AZIZ: Apologise to that!

MR HASSAN: You can't talk to me like that in my own property.

HASSAN: It's my property!

MR HASSAN: Shut up!

SANJAY: Gentlemen!... Gentlemen!... Don't let me be the cause of more bother... There's enough to be getting on with as it is... There's not a single thing that you lot can say that I've not heard before...so, don't you worry your little heads about a bloody thing... To some extent I take great joy in it, really... To me you are all just silly little boys who allow your throbbing testosterone to stimulate your aggressiveness into actually believing that this is your world...and that I just somehow exist in it... But you see... I have the strength of self-awareness and perspective on my side…showing me exactly who is in control… And you…you are nothing but unenlightened fools… just burly lads that are destined to continue talking shit whilst turning me on with your rough and tumble disagreements…never coming to any real conclusions but just slowly fulfilling my darkest fantasies.

MR BROWN: Fucking hell!… Where did it all go wrong, hey? When and where did it all go wrong? It all used to be so simple when I was a kid… Black and white, if you like… There was none of you…and I had no hate… I was happy –

SANJAY: Gay?

MR BROWN: Yes!… I was gay!… We were all gay!… Before you lot came about…we were all gay.

MR HASSAN: Don't be silly, Mr Brown…they were always about…the world is getting smaller, that's all…the world is getting smaller.

SANJAY: So, you once had a heart?

MR BROWN: Had a heart?… I fought for my fellow man, I did… Sweated my guts out for him, I did…… I was a docker…like my old man…a Union member, I was…and not just any old member…but a white ticket holder…that meant something, that did…… I'd shape-up every day for tallying –

SANJAY: You what?

MR BROWN: Don't worry about it… Dockers' talk…… With our own bare hands, we dealt with our nation's trade… from what we ate to what we wiped our arses with…… And we stuck together… At any point any union member could call for a show of cards. What a beautiful sight that was… Arms held high…holding on to their pride. Of course, 'White ticket' holders would take precedence over those with 'Blue tickets'…oh yes… And boy did we strike… We stuck together and fought for our own kind…… Then…you lot turn up… Start organizing your own groups… Changing everything… The way things looked… The way things sounded… The way things smelt… It all changed…… Then some of our leaders came out and spoke the truth… I say 'our leaders'…my old man went mental when I voted Tory… So did some of my work pals… But I knew we were right then and I know that we're right now…… It's British jobs for British workers… D'you hear me?… British jobs for British workers!

HAMID: Yes…but it all depends on what you consider British.

Pause.

HASSAN: I'm British.

Slight pause.

SANJAY: I'm British.

Slight pause.

JAMILLIA: I'm British.

DAVID: I'm British.

Slight pause.

MR HASSAN: I'm British.

HAMID: I'm British.

Slight pause.

ABDUL AZIZ: I'm British.

AISHA: I'm British

MR BROWN: Fucking hell!…… We can't all be British!

MR HASSAN: Well… European…

HAMID: It's all the same shit.

MR BROWN: No it fucking isn't!

HASSAN: No… I don't think it is.

MR BROWN: I mean, it's no good for any of us, is it?… All this bloody multiculturalism.

MR HASSAN: I don't know…it's not that bad.

MR BROWN: Not that bad!?… Multiculturalism, mate…is a painful death that slowly eats away at your character… killing everything that makes you 'you'…until there's nothing left of 'you'…till all you are is one big mass of compromise…… The pacified man.

HASSAN: The pacified man!?

MR BROWN: Yes!… The pacified man!… I mean tell me if I'm wrong… When we first get together we all desperately try to show the other who we are and how we won't change… therefore being right racist bastards… Which of course falls very uncomfortable with the other –

MR HASSAN: Well, kind of –

HASSAN: No, let him finish.

MR BROWN: Then of course we start having troubles, at which point all shit kicks off… So we start to look for the middle ground…somewhere where we still feel like ourselves but where we feel we are making concessions. I mean how bloody nice of us! And it works, things get a lot better, we all start to get on. Finding the middle ground leads to conciliation. It all starts looking hunky-dory…it's culture! Before we know it, conciliation through finding 'the middle ground' leads to you lot wanting more negotiation, more give and take. Which leads to more trouble, which leads back to reconciliation through more negotiation. Which inevitably leads to nothing but fucking pacification! Henceforth, we have the pacified man.

Slight pause.

HASSAN: My God, we talk some shit, don't we?

DAVID: I really do wish I never came in here.

MR BROWN: I mean, do you know how many times we've stopped you before…from pacifying us!… You want to read?… Read about that King Sobieski of Poland…who in 1683 smashed the forces of your Ottoman Empire who were pounding Vienna…the key to Europe!… He defeated you Muslims with such an impact that your Islamic world never attempted another military assault on Europe again…… That is until now!… Oh, we kept the might of the Ottoman Empire at bay… But when the clan of a zillion zillion Hassans come politely knocking on the door…it's all 'come in and make yourself at home, my dears'!

MR HASSAN: The Ottoman Empire –

MR BROWN: Oh, Ottoman shmottaman!… If it wasn't for European Christian culture civilising the world even America would still be full of nomadic tribes stuck in the Stone Age hunting for buffalo!… Although, one could argue they're not that different now, really.

HAMID: Civilising the world?!… What about the Spanish Inquisition?!

DAVID: What about Hitler?

MR BROWN: Well, he had to do something about the enemy within… Now!… Is anyone going to move that fucking Mercedes?!!

MR HASSAN: No!!

MR BROWN: Right!!

Once again, MR BROWN runs out of the patio doors quickly followed by everyone except MRS HASSAN and JAMILLIA, who calmly proceeds to pour more alcohol into the teapot. As she does this, we see the erect Mercedes go up in flames through the glass back wall.
Enter MR BROWN and the other characters.

MR HASSAN: He's crazy!… He's fucking crazy!!

MR BROWN: Yeah… I'm crazy!… I'm fucking mad, I am! Don't worry he'll buy you another car!… And if something happens to that one…he'll fucking buy you another!!… But what about me, hey?!!… Where's my Mercedes?!!!

HASSAN: Mr Brown…you're going red in the face again.

MR BROWN is once again bright red in the face and gasping for breath.

DAVID: You want to see him from this angle…he's got that big blue vein throbbing away like last time.

HASSAN: You really want to take it easy, Mr Brown.

SANJAY: Poor love.

DAVID: You've really got to calm down, mate.

HASSAN: A glass of water for Mr Brown, Sanjay.

SANJAY: Of course.

MR HASSAN: No…leave it, Sanjay.

HASSAN: What?

MR HASSAN: Leave it.

HASSAN: What a'you on about, baba?

MR HASSAN: Well like the man said… you've got to do something about the enemy within…haven't you?

ABDUL AZIZ: That's right… One way or another…you have to do something about the enemy within.

HASSAN: No water?

SANJAY: He doesn't look that bad to me.

MR BROWN is having a convulsion on the floor.

HASSAN: Have you lot lost the plot or what?!… David!… Get him a fucking glass of water!

DAVID: What can I say, Mr Hassan……it's *bashert*.

HASSAN: It's what?!

DAVID: Fate, Mr Hassan… Fate.

HAMID: Kismet.

MR HASSAN: That's right…it's kismet.

AISHA: What Allah wills…will be.

HASSAN: Is no one going to help him?!

JAMILLIA: Screw him.

ABDUL AZIZ: Astaghfirullah.

They all watch as MR BROWN's convulsion slowly comes to a halt as he is about to breathe his last breath. As his voice begins to croak and his body gives in to what seems the inevitable, he suddenly sits up with a big intake of breath.

MR BROWN: You fucking foreign bastards!!

Suddenly, MR HASSAN grabs AISHA's Hijab from off her head and wraps it round MR BROWNs neck and begins to throttle him.
He is quickly assisted by ABDUL AZIZ and DAVID.
At the same time, HAMID quickly takes the cloth off the erotic statue with the same intent but, having been beaten to it, now places it over AISHA's head before anyone can see her.
Now the full grotesque nature of the statue is on display again.
MR BROWN kicks his last breath.

HASSAN: Fucking hell!!

Pause.

AISHA: Can we go and eat now?

HASSAN: What are we going to do?

AISHA: Go and eat?

HASSAN: Shut up!

Suddenly, we hear the rhythmic sound of the building site.

MR HASSAN: David?

DAVID: It's good timing......we're about to fill in the foundations.

HAMID: You'll have to get my Mercedes out first.

ABDUL AZIZ: The Mercedes is gone, abba...we'll get another.

DAVID: Right... I'll get it sorted.

HASSAN: Have you lot gone fucking insane!?... You're going to bury him under my extension?!

SANJAY: Do you have a better idea?......

Slight pause.

...... Exactly.

DAVID: Right...you wrap him up in something nice and tight... And I'll see to the Merc.

Suddenly, we hear sirens and the glass back wall is lit with the flashing lights of the emergency services.
Then, once again, we hear the electronic chime of 'Jerusalem' by William Blake.

AISHA: It's the front door.

HASSAN: I know it's the front door!... It's my bloody front door!

HAMID: Who do you think it can be?

HASSAN: I wonder!

ABDUL AZIZ: What are we going to do?

MR HASSAN: Don't answer it.

HASSAN: That's it...fuck 'em.

JAMILLIA: I don't think that will work, somehow.

HASSAN: I swear to fucking Christ...if I ever get out of this shit... I will never drink again!!

MR HASSAN: Fucking hell!!… Hassan…you don't have any…you know…evidence…of anything…in the house?

HASSAN: No, Baba…only a fucking dead body!

MR HASSAN: That's alright then.

Again, we hear an electronic chime of 'Jerusalem' by William Blake.

HASSAN: That's it!… We're fucked!!

MR HASSAN: Don't answer it… They'll go away, I tell you.

Again, we hear an electronic chime of 'Jerusalem' by William Blake.

HASSAN: I don't think so!

Promptly, we see POLICEMAN knocking on the patio doors. POLICEMAN is tall, handsome and of mixed-race.

MR HASSAN: Fucking hell!!… It's the police!!

DAVID: Quick!… Stick him behind the sofa!

HASSAN: Behind the sofa!?… What is this?!!… A fucking pantomime?!!

MR HASSAN: You got a better idea?

Again, we hear an electronic chime of 'Jerusalem' by William Blake as POLICEMAN knocks louder on the patio doors.

HASSAN: Right, boys and girls!…Quick!… Get him behind the sofa!

All, except MRS HASSAN, now lend a hand in placing MR BROWN behind the sofa.
Enter POLICEMAN from the patio doors as all our characters quickly huddle around the sofa.

POLICEMAN: Evening.

Slight pause.

ALL: Evening!!

POLICEMAN: Oh, I see.

HASSAN: You see what?

POLICEMAN: Muslims.

HASSAN: Hey?

POLICEMAN: Muslims… Members of our very own Islamic community…… Very nice.

HASSAN: Is it?

POLICEMAN: As-Salaamu Alaikum.

HASSAN: Hey?

POLICEMAN: As-Salaamu Alaikum.

Slight pause.

ALL: Alaikum salaam.

POLICEMAN: How lovely… And such a lovely home.

HASSAN: Thank you.

POLICEMAN: This is what it's all about…… That's what I keep telling the boys at the station.

HASSAN: What is what all about?

POLICEMAN: The changing face of our society……
The smells… The taste… The colours… The shapes of things to come.

HASSAN: Absolutely.

POLICEMAN: Although I must admit………the boys at the station…don't agree.

HASSAN: No?

MR HASSAN: Hassan…ask him what the fuck he wants.

POLICEMAN: I'm sorry, sir…what was that?

HASSAN: How can we help you officer?

POLICEMAN: Don't you worry about me, sir... I just happen
to be passing by and noticed a Mercedes sticking out of
your backyard.

HASSAN: Yeah... I'm sorry about that.

POLICEMAN: Don't you dare apologise, sir... Mistakes happen
all the time...... Kismet!... That's what it is... Kismet!

DAVID: Shit!

MR HASSAN: That's right, Hassan... It's Kismet... Nothing to
worry about... Stay nice and cool.

POLICEMAN: Wait a minute.

ALL: What?!!

POLICEMAN: You, sir.

DAVID: Me, sir?

POLICEMAN: Yes... You, sir.

DAVID: What?

POLICEMAN: You're Jewish.

DAVID: Am I?

ALL: Yes!!

POLICEMAN: How lovely.

DAVID: Is it?

POLICEMAN: Shalom aleichem.

Slight pause

ALL: Aleichem shalom.

POLICEMAN: This really is something... Somehow I knew
today would turn out just fine.

HASSAN: Fuck!

MR HASSAN: Just fine, Hassan…take it nice and easy…because everything is just fine.

POLICEMAN: You know… I should call all the other officers to come in and have a look.

ALL: No!!

POLICEMAN: I haven't come at an inconvenient time…have I?

ALL: Well?!

POLICEMAN: Everyone should see this……… Unfortunately… they wouldn't give a damn anyway… So, there's no point of calling them in.

ALL: Oh, well.

POLICEMAN: Instead… I should take you to them.

ALL: Hah?!

POLICEMAN: Look at you… You are a beacon of light to the rest of us… Illuminating the path to true cultural harmony.

ALL: Yeah?

POLICEMAN: Well, look at you… Muslim and Jew… Jew and Muslim.

ABDUL AZIZ: Astaghfirullah.

POLICEMAN: And it's not the first time, is it?… All one has to do is read books to know that.

AISHA: Finally… Someone who reads.

POLICEMAN: I'm sorry…who said that?

AISHA slowly puts her hand up.

AISHA: Hiya.

POLICEMAN: As-Salaamu Alaikum, sister.

AISHA: Alaikum salaam.

POLICEMAN: When this Europe was still in its Dark Ages...it was you Muslims and Jews that side by side were developing the world of literature...science...and...... art!......

POLICEMAN has suddenly noticed the erotic statue and is slightly disturbed.

...... I mean...all one has to do is look around this very home...and one can find plenty evidence of the influence of the Muslim and Jew.

ALL: Hmm!

POLICEMAN: Europe wouldn't have even come out of the Dark Ages if the Muslims and the Jews from the Islamic world hadn't translated classical Greek texts into Arabic that later was translated into Latin and helped Europe move into......

ALL: The Renaissance...

POLICEMAN: Well done. And now they have the cheek to tell you to have a renaissance... I mean if it wasn't for the Islamic world... the Greeks... and the Jews...... what would Europe be?... What would we have?

MR HASSAN: That's right......... Although, I don't like that bit about the Greeks.

POLICEMAN: Ooh...the Greeks played their bit, sir... it's all there in the books.

MR HASSAN: Yes, well, that book is probably a forgery too... written by a Mr Popalopolos.

POLICEMAN: That's not true... and not fair.

HASSAN: Shut up Baba.

MR HASSAN: I'm only joking!... Bloody hell!... This is still a free country, you know... They've made no rules yet about making jokes about each other!

POLICEMAN: I think you'll find they have, sir.

MR HASSAN: Have they?

HASSAN: Yep.

MR HASSAN: Shit!

POLICEMAN: I mean, come on…help me out.

ABDUL AZIZ: Who?

POLICEMAN: You… My Muslim brother… The truth is…the coexistence of Muslims and Jews goes all the way back to the time of the Prophet… 'peace be upon him' –

POLICEMAN is waiting for the repetition of this phrase.

ALL: Peace be upon him.

POLICEMAN: When he signed treaties with the Jews of Madinah…the first charter of the world and one of the most supreme political documents ever prepared by any human being…… Isn't that right?

DAVID: Yeah… Isn't that right… 'Abdul'?

Slight pause.

ABDUL AZIZ: Yes…that is right.

POLICEMAN: You see……… I do know my history… Don't I, 'Abdul'?

ABDUL AZIZ: Astaghfirullah.

POLICEMAN: The truth is…if you look at history…… Jews and Muslims aren't enemies…… You are cousins.

ABDUL AZIZ: Cousins!?

DAVID: That's right…we're cousins………one big extended family…all from our great-great-grandfathers…… Abraham… Isaac…and Moses… But let's face it, all families have their disputes…but at the end of the day…

who understands you better than family, hey?... Ain't that right, Abdul?

DAVID has put his arm around ABDUL AZIZ and given him a big kiss.

ABDUL AZIZ: Astaghfirullah.

DAVID: So...seeing as we're cousins......does that mean I can marry someone...say...like...... Jamillia?

ALL: No!!!!

ABDUL AZIZ: I know the Sufis are cousins of the Jews...... I mean, your son even looks like a Jew!

POLICEMAN: That's right... He does... He has that Semitic face.

MR HASSAN: My son?

HASSAN: Who!?

ABDUL AZIZ: You!!

DAVID: Muzzletov, Mr Hassan!

HASSAN: Shalom, David!... Shalom!!

POLICEMAN: It's a shame others can't be like you...... Instead of killing each other!

ABDUL AZIZ: Maybe it's because they stole our land!

HAMID: That's true.

DAVID: Our land?!... You're a Pakistani from Leeds!

ABDUL AZIZ: And you're a North London Jew from God knows where!

DAVID: Russia!

ABDUL AZIZ: Exactly!

DAVID and ABDUL AZIZ quickly pretend to hug each other.

POLICEMAN: Are you sure I'm not interrupting anything?

Slight pause.

JAMILLIA: Actually......you have come in on something.

ALL: Hah!!

POLICEMAN: I knew I probably had.

Slight pause.

JAMILLIA: We are all here to celebrate.

MR HASSAN: What is she talking about?

POLICEMAN: Celebrate?

JAMILLIA: Yes... Celebrate......

POLICEMAN: Celebrate what?

Slight pause.

JAMILLIA: Marriage.

POLICEMAN: Of cultures?

JAMILLIA: In a way.

POLICEMAN: And in what other way?

Slight pause.

JAMILLIA: My marriage...............to Hassan.

A roar of thunder.

ALL: Hah?!

JAMILLIA: My marriage.........to Hassan.

A roar of thunder.
Slight pause.

POLICEMAN: How beautiful...... I'm so sorry for barging in.

JAMILLIA: Not at all... It's nice to have you here...... Ain't
that right, Hassan?

MR HASSAN: Hassan!!?

HASSAN: That's right…yes…nice to have you here.

POLICEMAN: Oh, no… I wish I didn't have to be here……
This is your day… I'm afraid I'm only in the way.

JAMILLIA: Not at all… Listening to you only perpetuates our
sense of euphoria… Isn't that right, Hassan……

Slight pause.

… Hassan?!

HASSAN: Yes… That's right………it only…erm……
perpetuates it.

MR HASSAN: Hassan!

POLICEMAN: Really?

JAMILLIA: You are such a breath of fresh air to us.

POLICEMAN: To you?

JAMILLIA: The outsiders.

POLICEMAN: Are you?… The outsiders?

MR HASSAN: Hassan?!!

JAMILLIA: Yes…we are the outsiders…… Hassan?

HASSAN: Yeah…the outsiders… whatever.

HAMID: Jamillia!!

JAMILLIA: But it's OK…… The outsiders are always the
driving force in change… Hassan?!

HASSAN: Yes!…Yes!…The driving force in change!

POLICEMAN: How true.

JAMILLIA: Our strength is to look at things from a different
perspective…and then…hopefully…provide invaluable
insights.

POLICEMAN: How true.

MR HASSAN: Yes!… Lovely!…… What the hell is going on, Hassan?!

JAMILLIA: I mean…everyone is an outsider in one way or another… And it's times like this when we get to celebrate the coming together of our differences… the marriage of all influences

POLICEMAN: The marriage of all influences… I like that.

JAMILLIA: It's also a perfect time to rid ourselves of all our fears.

POLICEMAN: Fears?… Surely not.

JAMILLIA: Oh, yes… We all have our fears…… Take my sister, for instance…take our parents…like many Muslims…like all outsiders…like…everyone, really… We so want to belong but are forever being reminded that we don't…so we cling to a cliché of what we think we once were… We make clichés of ourselves…and of each other…that way the growing pains tend to be less painful –

HAMID: OK, Jamillia…you have made your point.

JAMILLIA: To some I am a second generation immigrant…not first generation British… Because our parents were incoming foreigners…we are branded foreign too… You see, by branding us this way we are kept in our place and have little chance of reaching any position of power… And our parents don't mind…because they too want us to stay foreign…to be forever what they are… What they don't realize…but you do, dear officer…is that with each generation comes 'change'…we 'evolve'! –

HAMID: OK!… We get it! –

JAMILLIA: And from here on…it will be our children's turn… to evolve –

HASSAN: Children!!

POLICEMAN: How lovely that you should say such words… However… I wonder if your children will really get the opportunity.

JAMILLIA: Excuse me?

POLICEMAN: To evolve…alas, they are in a land where they are reminded on a daily basis that they don't belong… Not really… Will they be able to work their way to the top?… To head this beautiful land of ours?… your children King or Queen?

HASSAN: 'A King Hassan'.

JAMILLIA: 'A Queen Jamillia'.

HASSAN: 'Now there's a thought…'

ALL: Astaghfirullah!

POLICEMAN: Unfortunately you are of the wrong family for that…if everyone in this land had equal rights in hope at least…and not be headed by a lottery of birth…you might not feel 'foreign'…or 'second generation' anything…but fully-fledged members of our society who can see their offspring rising to the top to make a difference… That is when you'll have a true sense of responsibility for this as your home…

But, we have to remember that it is not just you who suffers…the so-called 'indigenous' are damaged by such a system too…a system that defines them as ancient and resistant to change.

MR HASSAN: Excuse me… I'll have nothing said against the royal family, if that is what you are saying –

HASSAN: Oh, will you stop trying to be something you're not!

MR HASSAN: Kettle calling pot black!… Esek oglu esek!!

HASSAN: You just called me a son of a donkey!

Suddenly, there is an explosion from the Mercedes.

POLICEMAN: I'm sorry…but duty calls…… However… I will be back.

MR HASSAN: When?!… I mean… When?

HASSAN: Yeah…when?… 'Cause I think I'll need you.

POLICEMAN: And I you, my friend… And I you.

Exit the POLICEMAN through the patio doors.
Slight pause.

ABDUL AZIZ: I'm gonna kill you!

HASSAN: I never touched her!… I swear to God I never!… And no one can prove otherwise!

MR HASSAN: It's always you!… There's always something wrong happening because of you!

JAMILLIA: Is this wrong?

HASSAN: Nothing's wrong!

ABDUL AZIZ: I'm gonna kill you!

HASSAN: Listen!… I never touched her, alright!

JAMILLIA: It true… He never touched me.

HASSAN: It is?

JAMILLIA: Yes.

HASSAN: You see!!… I told you I never touched her!!

MR HASSAN: Hassan!!… What do you mean you are married?!… I am your father…and now you tell me!… Who else knew about this!?

SANJAY: No one… It was a surprise to us all, believe me.

HAMID: I don't understand.

MR HASSAN: You and me both!… You don't get married, just like that!

HASSAN: No…you don't understand… It was a mistake.

JAMILLIA: A mistake?

MR HASSAN: Start explaining, Hassan.

HASSAN: Well, you see…… I don't really remember what happened.

MR HASSAN: What do you mean, you don't remember?!… Getting married is something you don't forget…believe me!

HASSAN: Well, I was drunk.

ABDUL AZIZ: You were drunk?!… Astaghfirullah!

HASSAN: I'm allergic to drink, you see……and…well… I don't remember.

SANJAY: Acute episodic paroxysmal alcoholic amnesia.

MR HASSAN: Oh, that's rubbish… He's just a spoilt stupid idiot who can face no responsibility… His mother spoilt him.

HASSAN: My mother spoilt me?!

MR HASSAN: Taking him to expensive doctors just so they can tell us this rubbish… He's a lazy bum!… That's all!… I gave up on him a long time ago!

HASSAN: She only took me to those doctors so she could get away from you… She'd take any excuse to get away from you.

MR HASSAN: You do nothing!… All you have to do is pick up the rent and you don't even do that right… I have to run and correct your mess all the time… You're a spoilt mummy's boy!… That's all you are!

HASSAN: Spoilt mummy's boy!?… Look at her!… The only thing she's spoilt is her liver… I might well be a mummy's boy, baba…but I never had a mummy's boy's mum!… I'll tell you that for nothing!

SANJAY: No...instead, I ended up with you.

MR HASSAN: How can you get married and not remember a thing?!

DAVID: All he remembers is standing in front of some bloke with a big beard.

SANJAY: In a Mosque.

MR HASSAN & HAMID: Jesus Christ!!!

HAMID: Jamillia?

HASSAN: It's not her fault... It was my cousin's stag night, you see...and we all went to wish him well for marrying Sandra –

AISHA: Sandra?

HASSAN: It's OK...she's my first cousin... You see, my uncle Hassan married an English woman –

ABDUL AZIZ: Disgusting!

HASSAN: And, well, they came to an agreement, you see, that they'd name the boy after the father, Hassan, and that the girl –

MR HASSAN: Get to the point, Hassan!

HASSAN: Well, anyway...... It was my cousin Hassan's stag night and............well, I don't remember much else...... All I keep thinking about is cakes...... I don't know why!

JAMILLIA starts to take her head scarf off.

MR HASSAN: Cakes!!... You get married!... You don't remember nothing!... And all you can think about is cakes!!?

ABDUL AZIZ: Bloody hell!... You're worst than Aisha!!

AISHA: I am getting hungry, actually.

ABDUL AZIZ: Shut up!

JAMILLIA starts to unbutton her coat.

HASSAN: I know…… It's weird that… I don't usually have a sweet tooth –

AISHA: Oh, I do –

ABDUL AZIZ: Shut up.

HASSAN: But for some stupid reason I can't stop thinking about cakes……

JAMILLIA has taken her coat off to reveal that she is wearing a leotard and a silk sash on which is written 'Commiserations'.

… It's freaking me out……every time I think of her or talk to her I just want to munch on something sweet.

HAMID & ABDUL AZIZ: Jamillia!!

HASSAN: Oh, my God!!!

ABDUL AZIZ: What are you wearing?!

HASSAN: Oh, my God!!!

JAMILLIA: Remember?

HASSAN: You came out of a cake!!!

MR HASSAN: Are you gonna tell me a 'Hassan' has married a Kiss-a-gram…a tart that popped out of a cake?!!

HAMID: Don't you dare say that about my daughter!

MR HASSAN: What should I say?!… Is this how you brought her up?!!

HAMID: No it's not!

MR HASSAN: Is that what you've got in there as well…another pop-up-tart!?

HAMID: No, it's not!

ABDUL AZIZ: Aisha is nothing like Jamillia.

HAMID: Jamillia was always the rebellious one.

ABDUL AZIZ: We haven't seen her in months.

HASSAN: Haven't seen her in months?!

ABDUL AZIZ: No…she ran off.

MR HASSAN: Who ran off?

ABDUL AZIZ: Jamillia.

MR HASSAN: Why?

HAMID: She didn't want to marry Farrukh.

MR HASSAN: Who's Farrukh?

JAMILLIA: He's my cousin in Pakistan and I don't know him from Adam.

HAMID: Who's Adam?

MR HASSAN: And what's wrong with marrying your cousin?

JAMILLIA & HASSAN: A lot!!

HASSAN: 'Religious', you said… 'No contact with boys', you said… 'Contact her family', you said!

DAVID: Well, how was I supposed to know… I'm just the builder!… A nice Jewish boy!…. You married her.

HASSAN: And you had to call your family!… Why?

JAMILLIA: Because I wanted to.

HASSAN: Oh my God!… All that time we thought you was something else… Why didn't you say something?

JAMILLIA: You wouldn't let me… And anyway…you were painting me out to be such a perfect picture, how could I?…… Besides… I didn't want to.

HAMID: What about Farrukh?

JAMILLIA: Screw him!

ABDUL AZIZ: Astaghfirullah!

MR HASSAN: Right!… You heard your daughter…… My son never touched her… We'll get the whole thing annulled.

HAMID: Annulled?… They got married in a Mosque, this is in the eyes of God. This is no Kafir marriage…it's a Muslim one.

MR HASSAN: Ah!… Muslim, Shmuslim!… No son of mine is marrying a Wahhabi!

ABDUL AZIZ: And no sister of mine is marrying a Sufi!

HAMID: You know my grandfather was a Sufi.

ABDUL AZIZ: Abba!!… Now is not the time!

HAMID: But they're already married!

JAMILLIA: Is it all coming back to you now?

HASSAN: Bit by bit. Or should I say, slice by slice?

JAMILLIA: Your eyes…they're the first thing I noticed when I came out that cake… The way you were looking at me… not like the others… You didn't make me feel…cheap.

MR HASSAN: I'm telling you this will never work!

ABDUL AZIZ: I won't let it work!… Abba!… Say something!

HAMID: Well, the way I see it…one down…two to go…… I'm getting too old for this parent shit.

ABDUL AZIZ: Abba!!

JAMILLIA: All we did all night is talk… It was my first night on this job……but you made it a lot easier for me… We just talked… You made me laugh.

MR HASSAN: We are nothing like you!

ABDUL AZIZ: You're not wrong there!

MR HASSAN: I mean look at you!

ABDUL AZIZ: Look at us!?… Look at you!

MR HASSAN: We're from different worlds…… You're more –

ABDUL AZIZ: Islamic!

MR HASSAN: Eastern!… And we're more –

ABDUL AZIZ: Kafir!

MR HASSAN: European!

JAMILLIA: We ate…and we drank……and then we drank some more… We talked about our families…our cousins mostly… I told you about Farrukh…and you told me about the Peckham Hassans… I talked about Islam…and how it was the one thing that I felt comforted me while I wasn't seeing my family… And how I couldn't believe what I was doing…but that I needed the money……… You talked about……your extension.

MR HASSAN: What am I going to say to the family… 'A Hassan married a Wahhabi'?!

ABDUL AZIZ: Salafi!… Your son married a Salafi!

MR HASSAN: You say, 'Salafi'……we say, 'Wahhabi'.

ABDUL AZIZ: Let's call the whole thing off!

HAMID: But it's already happened!

MR HASSAN: My God!… Look at you!… Look at her!

ABDUL AZIZ: What about her?!

MR HASSAN: Don't you get hot in that thing?

AISHA: Sometimes…… But the fires of hell are hotter still, my dear brother.

MR HASSAN: Oh my God!!

JAMILLIA: We walked…and we talked……till the early hours…till we passed a Mosque that was open for morning prayers… We watched all the men going in as we listened to the call for prayer... Then one of them asked us...if we were going in...... Before he could see it I quickly grabbed the bottle of Jack Daniels that you were about to offer him......... And then you said... 'Why not'.

ABDUL AZIZ: I told you she was Selfish!... Selfish! Selfish! Selfish!

AISHA: I really am getting hungry, you know... Can we have more tea?

JAMILLIA: I sat there in the women's prayer area...you were only gone twenty minutes... You came and got me...and said...... 'Don't worry... Farrukh will never get his dirty claws on you'...... Another twenty minutes and we walked out of the Mosque...a married couple.

MR HASSAN: I knew there was something wrong when Sanjay said something was up!... I knew it!

DAVID: Look!

As she has been talking to him, JAMILLIA has worked her way over to HASSAN. They are now face to face and are about to kiss.

SANJAY: Master!!

ALL: Oh, shut up!!

HASSAN and JAMILLIA kiss.
SANJAY ascends the stairs and exits into their bedroom.

AISHA: Does this mean I can have Farrukh now?

Enter the POLICEMAN through the patio doors only to see JAMILLIA in her new state and in the arms of HASSAN.

POLICEMAN: Now that is what I call progressive...... But I'm afraid I'm interrupting again.

HASSAN: Not at all... You couldn't have come at a better time.

POLICEMAN: Unfortunately...the other officers and I will have to ask some questions.

MR HASSAN: And we will have to answer.

POLICEMAN: Just routine questions.

HAMID: Do we really have to talk to them?

POLICEMAN: Oh…they're not that bad…they're getting better, anyway…… And if you're walking down the right path…and you're willing to keep walking…eventually you'll make progress…… Surely then we'll all extend to greater things.

Slight pause.

JAMILLIA: Well……shall we?

JAMILLIA opens the patio doors.

MR HASSAN: Out there!… To all those policemen?

JAMILLIA: Of course… On the other hand…we could always invite them in…to sit round the sofa, say?

HASSAN: No!… Out there……would be perfect.

JAMILLIA: Then let's.

MR HASSAN: Yes…let's.

HAMID: Terrible how these accidents happen.

MR HASSAN: Yes…terrible.

AISHA: I'm starving.

ABDUL AZIZ: Shut up.

DAVID: I can't even remember why I came in here in the first place.

HASSAN: It was kismet.

DAVID: *Bashert.*

HASSAN: It don't matter what we call it. Where we're heading…it's all the same shit.

Exit ALL after HASSAN through the patio doors.
Again, we hear the rhythmic sound of the building site – the extension.
Pause.

EXCERPT FROM PRESIDENT OBAMA'S SPEECH TO THE TURKISH PARLIAMENT: Now, our two democracies are confronted by an unprecedented set of challenges. An economic crisis that recognizes no borders. Extremism that leads to the killing of innocent men, women and children. Strains on our energy supply and a changing climate. The proliferation of the world's deadliest weapons, and the persistence of tragic conflict.

These are the great tests of our young century. And the choices that we make in the coming years will determine whether the future will be shaped by fear or by freedom; by poverty or by prosperity; by strife or by a just, secure and lasting peace.

This much is certain: no one nation can confront these challenges alone, and all nations have a stake in overcoming them. That is why we must listen to one another, and seek common ground. That is why we must build on our mutual interests, and rise above our differences. We are stronger when we act together. That is the message that I have carried with me throughout this trip to Europe.

Enter SANJAY from the bedroom door on the upper floor. He is wearing a coat and is carrying a suitcase.
Standing on the upper floor, SANJAY looks around at what was once an immaculate home but now a complete mess.
After a moment, he picks up his suitcase and descends to the lower floor.
We hear the electronic chime of 'Jerusalem' by William Blake.
Enter HANDSOME YOUNG MAN with foreign accent. He is also carrying a suitcase.

HANDSOME YOUNG MAN: Hello… I've just arrived from Turkey… I'm sorry but the front door was open.

SANJAY: Of course.

HANDSOME YOUNG MAN: I was looking for my cousin, Hassan.

SANJAY: Your cousin?

HANDSOME YOUNG MAN: Yes... I'm sorry, my name is –

SANJAY: Don't tell me... 'Hassan'.

HANDSOME YOUNG MAN: How did you know?

SANJAY: Let's just say... I'm an old friend of the family.

HANDSOME YOUNG MAN: This is my cousin's home?

SANJAY: Yes... I'm ashamed to say.

HANDSOME YOUNG MAN: I'm very surprised... It's a real mess.

SANJAY: Yes...... Things have been a little too...cluttered lately.

HANDSOME YOUNG MAN: He has a lot of books, though... that is good...a home is always richer for it.

SANJAY: If you say so.

HANDSOME YOUNG MAN: You live here too?

SANJAY: I used to... It was my job to keep it all in good shape...but as you can see...that's all over now...... You staying nearby?

HANDSOME YOUNG MAN: Yes... I'm just moving into a place down the road......... I will need someone to keep that nice and...'in shape'.

SANJAY: I'll have to give you my résumé.

HANDSOME YOUNG MAN: That will be nice.

SANJAY: I tell you what...let's walk out together and you can tell me all about you.

Arm in arm, SANJAY and the HANDSOME YOUNG MAN exit.
As the lights are about to fade, MR BROWN slowly rises from behind
the sofa.

CURTAIN.